99 Names of God

99 Names of God

David Steindl-Rast

With Calligraphies by Shams Anwari-Alhosseyni

ORBIS BOOKS
Maryknoll, New York 10545

Founded in 1970, Orbis Books endeavors to publish works that enlighten the mind, nourish the spirit, and challenge the conscience. The publishing arm of the Maryknoll Fathers and Brothers, Orbis seeks to explore the global dimensions of the Christian faith and mission, to invite dialogue with diverse cultures and religious traditions, and to serve the cause of reconciliation and peace. The books published reflect the views of their authors and do not represent the official position of the Maryknoll Society. To learn more about Orbis Books, please visit our website at www.orbisbooks.com.

English edition copyright © 2021 by Orbis Books.

Published by Orbis Books, Box 302, Maryknoll, NY 10545-0302.
All rights reserved.

Originally published as *99 Namen Gottes* © 2019 Verlagsanstalt Tyrolia, Innsbruck, Austria. English translation by Peter Dahm Robertson.

Unless otherwise stated, all poetry translations © 2021 by Peter Dahm Robertson. The Scripture quotations contained herein are from the New Revised Standard Version: Catholic Edition, Copyright © 1989 and 1993, by the Division of Christian Education of the National Council of the Churches of Christ in the United States of America. Used by permission. All rights reserved.

No part of this publication may be reproduced or transmitted in any form or by any means, electronic or mechanical, including photocopying, recording, or any information storage or retrieval system, without prior permission in writing from the publisher.

Queries regarding rights and permissions should be addressed to: Orbis Books, P.O. Box 302, Maryknoll, NY 10545-0302.

Manufactured in the United States of America

Library of Congress Cataloging-in-Publication Data

Names: Steindl-Rast, David, author. | Dahm Robertson, Peter, translator. | Anwari-Alhosseyni, Shams, illustrator. | Steindl-Rast, David. 99 Namen Gottes.
Title: 99 names of God / David Steindl-Rast ; trans. Peter Dahm Robertson ; with calligraphies by Shams Anwari-Alhosseyni.
Other titles: 99 Namen Gottes. English | Ninety-nine names of God
Description: Maryknoll, New York : Orbis Books, [2021] | Summary: "99 Names of God offers a meditation on each of the 99 names of God that are found in the Islamic creed"— Provided by publisher.
Identifiers: LCCN 2020043530 (print) | LCCN 2020043531 (ebook) | ISBN 9781626984226 (trade paperback) | ISBN 9781608338856 (epub)
Subjects: LCSH: God (Islam) | God—Name—Meditations.
Classification: LCC BP166.2 .S7313 2021 (print) | LCC BP166.2 (ebook) | DDC 297.2/112—dc23
LC record available at https://lccn.loc.gov/2020043530
LC ebook record available at https://lccn.loc.gov/2020043531

Contents

The word "God"...   7

The 99 Names   10

HE lets Himself be glimpsed in the letters   209

Endnotes   213

Biographies   219

The word "God" . . .

. . . stems from human history's most consequential discovery. It is a prehistoric artifact, which, even today, glows red-hot from the fires that smelted it in the forge of mystical experience. The insight that enlightened our ancient, only just human ancestors was that we stand in a personal relationship with the unfathomable mystery of life, indeed of the cosmos, of all of reality. And that we may call to that mystery, because it calls to us. This word "call to," with its meaning of invocation, marks the etymological root of the word "God." It is not a name, but rather a reference to our relationship with the nameless; it is not a term for some creature, but rather points to the origin by which all creatures originally sprang from non-being into being. In short, it is a word with the momentous task of pointing to the mystery.

Mystery, in this absolute sense, is not a vague term. It means that deepest reality which we can never take hold of, but may understand if we let it take hold of us. This distinction between taking hold of—that is, grasping, or comprehending—and being taken hold of—that is, being touched, or understanding—is familiar to us all from our experiences with music: We cannot take hold of its nature, cannot grasp or define it in concrete terms, cannot comprehend it intellectually. And yet we can understand it in the moment in which the music touches us—takes hold of us. Being touched from within allows us an understanding—that is, "standing

7

within"—that goes beyond any comprehension or grasping, which always approaches things from the outside. That experience in music applies to the Mystery as well. And it is especially through music that the Great Mystery can often touch us. However, any other touching experience can work just as well, since the Great Mystery is the reason for and foundation of all experience.

Being touched, words fail us. We fall silent beneath the vaulted, starry sky. The vast grandeur of nature in all its freedom is overwhelming. When we look through a window, however, things are different; then nature seems familiar, something we can get a handle on. Through the names of God, we can contemplate the supernal mystery as through windows—otherwise we would have to fall silent. It is human comprehension which determines the shape of these windows and limits their size. None of them can show everything, and no two of them show the exact same picture. For this reason alone, it is worth getting to know the names of God in other religious traditions. Nowadays, there is a far weightier additional reason: All too often, one partial view is played off against another, name against name, to the point of mutual bloodshed.

Reverential encounter with the names of God in Islam, therefore, can be of great significance to Christians. Even merely paying attention to them can signal a readiness for dialog—and what could be more necessary today than dialog? It may be what our collective survival depends on. For that reason, I have delved into a traditional list of the 99 names of Allah, contemplating one name after another, and collecting my thoughts into this book. In turn, I hope that my reflections will encourage readers to reflect. Here, images as well as words seek to inspire reflection. The calligraphies depicting the individual names offer an opportunity for silently immersing oneself in their forms and so coming nearer to the silent mystery than one could with words alone.

Now that I hold it in my hands, I am filled with gratitude for this book. Through his masterful calligraphy, my friend Shams Anwari-Alhosseyni has made it more valuable than I could have ever imagined. Those who follow my reflections with heart and mind can now also follow the silent message reflected in the letters—and so it has become doubly a book of reflections. The joy of reflection is also, not least, made possible by the pleasing design of the book. For this, I thank all the staff of Tyrolia publishing, especially graphic designer Martin Caldonazzi and my editor and friend, Klaus Gasperi, who in addition to his many helpful suggestions for the text also did great services in rendering the layout of each page. For valuable advice, my thanks go out to Prof. Maria M. Jaoudi-Smith, Prof. Brigitte Kwizda-Gredler, Prof. Reinhard Nesper and Heidimaria Stauber, Dr. Hortense Reintjens-Anwari, and Alberto Rizzo with Lizzie Testa. The counsel and encouragement of these faithful friends have supported me again and again over the past decade of work.

This book of reflections is dedicated to the people—of any and all religious denominations—who dare to pass through the gates of the many different names of God into the one nameless Mystery that unites us all.

—Brother David Steindl-Rast, OSB
on the hacienda *La Güelta de Areco*
near Azcuenaga in the Pampas,
Argentina, March 2019

1 ar-Raḥmaan
the MOST GRACIOUS

"All is grace," says Augustine. Everything we have is given to us as a gift. Joyous gratefulness and grateful joy spring from this insight. But truly admitting that everything—really, everything there is—is a gift requires joyfully recognizing that there is nothing I have that comes from my own power. Like fallow land waiting to be ploughed, harrowed, and seeded; like a field dependent on rain and sun, from birth, I am dependent on others and on life circumstances over which I have no control. My very existence is pure gift. That gift can be an inexhaustible wellspring of joy, as long as I continually recall it to my memory. That is why the German poet Matthias Claudius exhorts us "to sing daily":

> I thank the Lord, as joyful as a child on Christmas
> morning
> That I may be!, and have this human visage me
> adorning.[1]

My reflections on how poor I am on my own can thus grow into joy—joy in the fact that the poverty of those who recognize their own poverty shall be filled with overflowing riches by the MOST GRACIOUS. This insight then makes us willing—even eager—to give to others from the bounty we have ourselves been given. Whenever we call God the MOST GRACIOUS and are conscious of the fact that all is gift and grace, the longing grows within us to be gracious to others and to act with grace toward all who need it.

Of all the things I have been given, what is most valuable to me? What gift of mine can I pass on as a gift to someone else today? Isn't the greatest gift I can make to everyone I meet my joy in living?

2 ar-Raḥeem
the MOST MERCIFUL

When we give God this second name, we are not actually adding anything to the first, but consciously applying it to our own relationship with God: God the Most Gracious is the MOST MERCIFUL unto me personally. God gazes upon me as a mother on her child. In addition to the good, she sees clearly all that is not yet good, and she is merciful. That is, her maternal heart feels the pain the child is inflicting on itself whenever it rejects something of life. For "good" means "life-affirming," and only those things that (still) resist life's harmonious flowering can be called "evil."

In her heart, the mother feels the pain of which the child itself may be still barely conscious, and she suffers. Only mothers know this kind of compassion. It is a different form of labor pains. Just as the labor pains once gave the child life, so this mercy now longs to give the child fullness of life. Mercy shines in the mother's eyes as a light, a light that encourages beyond what words of encouragement could ever say.

It is the same with God's maternal gaze. It does not sugarcoat, nor does it judge. It gives me courage and creates a space into which I can grow; space in which all that is not yet good can blossom fully into the good. Only the MOST MERCIFUL can let my heart bloom in such a way.

Today, can I look through those maternal eyes at everything that isn't yet good? If I succeed, I may see whatever I have looked at in the light of mercy grow and blossom unexpectedly. New, creative solutions appear. Won't you too try to see "evil" as "not yet good"?

3 al-Malik
the KING

It is doubly dangerous to call God KING. First, it might suggest ascribing to God qualities that often characterize worldly kings. This would be a serious mistake. Kings boast, whereas God's workings are hidden. Kings oppress; God empowers. Kings enforce obedience; God gives the gift of freedom.

Kingship stands for the highest rank of authority in a power system whose fundamental principles threaten to destroy our world. This second reason makes it even more dangerous to give God the name of KING. When we do so without thinking, it is too easy to become numb to the contradiction between the royal and the divine systems of power. And yet this contradiction is absolute.

Wherever we may live in the world, our daily experience makes us all too familiar with the system of power from which the name KING originates. That system is our society's power hierarchy, a pyramid built from countless smaller pyramids of the same kind. They all are marked by violence, competition, oppression, and exploitation. Whoever is at the top is considered the king.

In contrast, where does our experience of divine power come from? We sense it in the order of the universe and in the way that the Great Mystery we call God works in nature. Instead of a pyramid of power, we find a network of networks; instead of violence, an interplay for the good of the whole. Even those things that seem at first glance to be cruel competition fit into the larger whole and contribute to the harmonious balance. Instead of rivalry and oppression, we find mutual give and take; instead of exploitation, sharing. In the universe, God is KING in the sense of an organizing power that pervades all things. But we must never blur the distinction between these two forms of power.

Either God is KING or the potentates of this world are. Whoever calls God KING—and acts accordingly—is radically challenging the existing power system and in the end rejecting the authority of those in power. In some places, that can cost you your life, but almost everywhere, it endangers, at the very least, your social standing. Calling God KING requires courage—courage for a wholly new world order.

Is God my KING, or do I actually treat my boss and the existing power system as my highest authority?

4 al-Quddúus
the HOLY ONE, the Absolutely Pure

In peak experiences, such as witnessing the birth of a child, or listening to a unique concert performance, or spending a beautiful day in the mountains, or standing beneath the vaulted sky of a starlit night, we can simultaneously be fascinated and shaken by the feeling of a presence that commands reverence. We may then give this mysterious Thou awaiting us in the encounter the name of the HOLY ONE.

When we are simultaneously fascinated and in awe of something, we call it holy. This must be how the sea seems to a small child running down the beach toward the water with shrieks of joy, and then immediately drawing back from the wave breaking in a crash of foam. As adults, we can feel something similar when some holy sight, such as the silhouette of the Cheops pyramid against the night sky, enraptures us but at the same time fills us with an emotion almost like fear at its transcendence.

A person's inner nobility can almost be measured by how strongly such holiness touches their heart. The thrill of an encounter with something transcendent can cause in us a longing: we too want to become so noble, live such an undistorted life. This striving for pure sincerity can be the beginning of a holy (that is, whole) life. Wholeness and holiness are connected by the conception of sincere, unbroken oneness.

The HOLY ONE is simultaneously the healing, the merciful of the earlier name. We must never forget that holiness and mercy go together. In the encounter with the HOLY ONE, I become conscious not only of my own flawed nature, but also of the grace by which the Absolutely Pure, the Whole turns toward me and makes me—yes me, just as I am—holy. Passing on this gift of mercy to all I encounter is true purity, true holiness, true reverence to the HOLY ONE. Just as a clean windowpane lets sunlight stream through undimmed, so I can let the mercy of the HOLY ONE stream through me.

Today, what opportunities do I have to show reverence to the HOLY ONE by letting pure mercy stream through me? Yes, this honoring task is meant for me. So on whom or on what can I shine the healing rays of the HOLY ONE by being merciful myself, today?

5 as-Salaam
the PEACE, the Giver of Peace

What is peace? Is it not—as Western philosophy in the Middle Ages understood it, *tranquilitas ordinis*—the silent calm arising from order? Of course, we should not think of it as "silent as the grave," or of a judge shouting, "Order!" in a noisy courtroom. PEACE is much closer to the dynamic stillness of a calmly burning candle flame and is rooted in an all-encompassing order, the ordering principle of which is love: love as a lived Yes to mutual belonging of all to all.

Understood this way, peace is far more than a historical period without war. True PEACE means that the whole fullness of being can unfold harmoniously. Just as in music a composer's skill combines consonant and dissonant chords to form a higher harmony, the divine PEACE can bridge and resolve all contradictions and opposition. Even discord and unanimity, taken together, serve a higher unity. And from this perspective, we may call God PEACE.

This peace can be felt not only in quiet times of tranquil stillness, but particularly when, in our public or our private lives, "skies are lightning-rent," as Joseph von Eichendorff writes:

Beat on, ye wings of fire!
When skies are lightning-rent
Then stands with knightly ire
My spirit, battle-bent.

Sky lit and forest roaring
The soul truly elate;
It greets, freely adoring,
The true, the grave, the great.

As on a boundless ocean
the thoughts so widely roam:
The sails hold fast their motion
Howe'er the waves may foam.

Lord God, my days and wonder
are watchéd by Thy will.
Knowing it shall not founder
My heart grows calm and still.[2]

When I feel "my heart grow calm and still," I have found my personal mooring from which to enter into the PEACE of God. Where can I find such a mooring in my everyday life, in the swell of the waves or the billow of the sails? It is easy to miss, but invaluable once we discover it.

6 al-Mu'min
the STEADFAST, the Preserver of Security

Belief, in its deepest meaning, does not mean to believe something (that is, to consider it true). Instead, it means believing *in*, trusting in God as the STEADFAST. In biblical Hebrew, the rock-solid steadfastness of God and our faithful trust in God are described by one and the same word. This word *emunah* (אֱמוּנָה), just like the word al-Mu'min, the STEADFAST, comes from a root meaning "steadfast, solid, reliable." The word "Amen" comes from the same root, and can be seen as the seal that our faith stamps on this mutual relationship of divine steadfastness and human reliance on God.

And so it is no coincidence that, for all traditions going back to Abraham as the father of the faith, "Amen" became a central, essential word. When the three Amen-traditions—the Jewish, the Christian, and the Islamic—say "Amen," they are affirming their faith in God the STEADFAST, their joint faith. In this spirit, Psalm 41 ends with an emphatic Amen:

Blessed be the Lord, the God of Israel,
from everlasting to everlasting.
Amen and Amen. (Psalm 41:13)

A Christian hymn rightly links the word "Amen" with the steadfastness and fidelity ("troth") of God, by beginning with the words:

> Amen! Amen! Amen ever
> From the mouth of God resounds,
> Carrying that name forever,
> that His troth in all abounds.[3]

And Muhammad al-Bukhari, a ninth-century Islamic scholar, wrote: "When the imam says *ameen*, then say ye *ameen*, for when his *ameen* joins with the *ameen* of the angels, then the sins of the past shall be forgiven."

Do I know anybody from one of the other Amen-traditions? Today, might I find a chance to speak with one of them about how closely and personally the word "Amen" connects us in our faith? And if I know only people from my own tradition, how might I get to know someone from another tradition? The state of the world today requires it.

7 al-Muhaymin
the GUARDIAN and Keeper

From what is God the GUARDIAN actually guarding me? Certainly not from the blows of fate, which hit all of us, whether we place ourselves under God's guardianship or it never even occurs to us to do so. And yet, all who flee from the heat of life's hardest moments into the protective shade of God attest to the fact that under the guard of God, they were able to cool their heads and breathe easy. So what, then, does that difference consist of?

Whether or not we know ourselves to be guarded by God, the external circumstances remain the same. What stands the test is our inner attitude of trust—not because we are fooling ourselves and telling ourselves what we want to hear. No! Our trust in God is proved right because it guards us from desperation. Desperation makes us blind to the possibilities that, despite everything, are still open to us. Trust, however, opens our eyes and lets us discover unsuspected paths forward. In this, God reveals himself as the GUARDIAN. He works upon us not "from the outside in," but from the innermost depth of the Mystery in which our life is rooted.

Who around me is having a particularly difficult time right now and may need my guardianship? Instead of talking about the GUARDIAN, let us silently enter into the protective shade of the divine Mystery together.

8 al-Azeez
the ALMIGHTY, the Venerable

Once again, this is a divine name that can easily mislead us. Even the word "might" resonates with too many tones of abuse of power, oppression, exploitation, and the like. And to extend this into almightiness, utterly boundless power? Our fundamental human faith senses a fullness of power we want to refer to when we call God the ALMIGHTY—but one which has nothing in common with the power of human rulers.

Again and again, people show their love of power. But with God, it is about the power of love. Only love deserves to be called almighty. Why? Because there is nothing—truly, absolutely nothing—that love cannot transform and turn to good. Power, then, is not simply an attribute of God the ALMIGHTY. Rather, God is almightiness because God is love.

Can you think of a truly loving person? That could be a person from whom—by observing, not by speaking—you can learn why God is called the ALMIGHTY.

9 al-Jabbar
the POWERFUL

Perhaps we should call God not the POWERFUL, but simply power. Whatever we imagine when hearing this name is, after all, an image. A precious image, but still an image. And like all the 99 names, it remains only one way of indicating God's nameless reality. Yes, even the name "God" is only a word for the unnamable reality to which the word points us. How do we experience this in the end unnamable reality we call "God"? As a power, a power acting on everything. The millions who go to Alcoholics Anonymous meetings testify to the "Higher Power" to which they have entrusted themselves and that enables them to do what otherwise seemed impossible.

Any person knows what is meant by the phrase "the power of life"—on all levels, from the bodily to the highest spiritual realm. Is our own power of life not itself an experience of that "higher power"? And the more science learns about how living things "work," the more mysterious we find the origins and nature of the power of life. In the end, by calling God the POW-ERFUL, we are not ascribing to him some trait. Instead, we are reverentially pointing to that "Higher Power" that acts within us and yet remains forever unfathomable.

Today, take the time to look long and quietly at something alive—perhaps a sleeping child, a tree, your own hand. As you do, silently speak the words "the POWERFUL" and contemplate what you imagine behind them.

10 al-Mutakabbir
the TRANSCENDENT,
the Supreme, the Majestic

What do you experience as transcendent? Snow-covered mountain peaks? An ancient olive tree? The vaulted heights of a Gothic cathedral? And what does your soul experience when it encounters the transcendent? In the words of the German poet, Joseph von Eichendorff, "it greets, freely adoring / the true, the grave, the great." When we call God the TRANSCENDENT, we are speaking of truth, of gravity, and of greatness. In this context, greatness means that we feel humility before the TRANSCENDENT.

Humility, yes, but in no way humiliation. Quite the opposite. We feel that precisely in this humility lies our highest dignity. For the encounter with the TRANSCENDENT fills us with a gravity, a seriousness that is celebratory but not theatrical, since everything about it is true. In fact, how "true" we ourselves are depends on whether and how deeply we are capable of being touched by the transcendent. Only very few other feelings refer so directly to something inexpressible, something final. That is why we call God the TRANSCENDENT.

Do you sometimes have a chance to stand and gaze up at the starry night sky? Even if you don't, you can always close your eyes and think about the fact that there are as many stars in the universe as grains of sand on all the beaches of the world combined. At that thought, are you not standing in the presence of the TRANSCENDENT?

11 al-Khaaliq
the CREATOR

This divine name forms a trinity with the two following names. Their meanings are interwoven, and so it is not particularly important to distinguish the Origin and the Shaper from the CREATOR. All these names are like the darkened glass that children hold up to their eyes to observe an eclipse of the sun without being blinded: they give us only a sense of the nameless light that shines upon us in each name of God.

This sense, expressed in the name of CREATOR, arises in us when we see the beauty of the world and discover the order that governs the natural world down to its minutest parts. The artist in us automatically thinks of the creativity of an outstanding master, while the scientist in us cannot stop marveling at the sheer power expressed there. What impresses us so much is the creative power of a higher reality, which we therefore call CREATOR. But we must not take our poetic imagery literally, not even the image of the CREATOR. As we have said, God does not act on the world "from outside." Instead, the name CREATOR points to the magnitude of the Mystery from whose creative power all that is given proceeds.

What is your area of creativity? Maybe today you can bake a cake or repair a bicycle. The more we discover our own creative power and experience it as a gift—that is, as something given, and as a responsibility to fulfill—the closer we get to the nature of the CREATOR.

12 al-Baari'
the ORIGIN

The root of this Arabic name of God is the same as that of the Hebrew word for "create," which can be used only of God. As human beings, we can work creatively only with what has already been created, with what is already there. But how is it that there is anything at all, rather than nothing? As children, we were still able to wonder and ask questions like this. Such wonderings, which Plato calls the beginnings of all philosophical thought, give rise to the question of the ORIGIN of all things.

Etymologically, the word "ORIGIN" comes from the image of rising or leaping forth. What is this leap? Being leaps into existence from non-being. Now, the saying that tells us that "nothing will come of nothing" is quite right—yet the wellspring of all being is only "nothing" in the sense that it is "not something." But it is not an empty void. This divine nothing which the German poet, Angelus Silesius, in his mystical seventeenth-century epigram, calls "overnought" is the maternal foundation, pregnant with boundless possibilities. The ORIGIN, then, is that leap from possibility to reality, from pure "Could-Be" into "So-Being."

> *The tender godhead is a nought and overnought.*
> *Who sees in all but nought—man, best believe!—*
>   *he sees.*[4]

Sees what? The divine reality in all things: the Great Mystery, encompassing both poles of the ORIGIN, being and non-being in one and at the same time the leap itself. The name Creator points more to being, and the name ORIGIN more to the leap from out of non-being. Yes, in everything we look at, we can learn to "see" the Great Mystery as well, to truly feel it as the nothing behind the origin—as if as a background. In the same way, we can learn to listen to the silence in which we are hearing the music: not as something additional to the music, but as its precondition.

As a child, you—like all children—were a young philosopher. Can you find the way back, not to simple-mindedness, but to this simplicity? Trust yourself, and then carefully reread these reflections on the name of the ORIGIN.

13 al-Muṣṣawwir
the SHAPER, the Fashioner

All the names we give God are like bridges between what can be named and what cannot. We must succeed in viewing both bridgeheads at once. Looking only at the unnamable light would make us blind. But seeing only the nameable would be shortsighted. Only if they enthrall and thrill us at the same time can we realize that Creator and Origin—being and non-being—refer to one and the same Ultimate Reality. In other words, in the river, we recognize the wellspring and in the wellspring the river—but we recognize its true power only when we give ourselves up to its current. And this current SHAPES: it alters the form of the world as a torrent moves mountain rocks. Through all, good or ill, that happens to us, the SHAPER fashions us into our shape, but only to the extent that we allow it to happen. At first and at our innermost, we are at one with the Great Mystery. We experience the SHAPER as our own innermost yearning to shape our lives.

Can you feel something within you that wants to change? Change can be painful—but it feels good to be aware that our lives aren't shaped by our resistance to external forces, but by what we let happen.

14 al-Ghaffar
the ALL-FORGIVING

In the end, with each name of God, we mean the one to whom all things refer: the Giver. This giving is so boundless that it naturally includes the highest form of giving, which is to say forgiving. That is why we call God the ALL-FORGIVING. We arrive at this insight not just by reasoning, but through our practical experience. As soon as we truly forgive harm that is done to us, it is healed—not gone, but transformed. What used to burn us, warms us; warms our own heart and the heart of the person who did us harm.

But what does forgiveness mean? It means giving so completely that we give away ourselves, that is, the accuser. By doing so, we no longer stand opposed to the other who has made us suffer, but become one with them. And this new "One" now, as we say, "takes this wrong upon him- or herself," and thereby lifts it—in the fullest sense of the word "lift." This is what the ALL-FORGIVING does with us.

Where are you still hurt by unforgiven harm that was done to you? Will you forgive it today? You can be certain that you will experience the transformation brought by forgiveness. That is part of reality's deepest nature.

15 al-Qahhar
the Subduer, the One who has the UPPER HAND

In our imagination, the name UPPER HAND conjures up images of battles or arguments, in which one side gains the upper hand. But when we use UPPER HAND as the name of God, it cannot be a matter of battles, and certainly not of two sides. God, after all, is on both sides, on all sides. And God does not need to fight and vanquish. The highest and Ultimate Reality has the UPPER HAND from the beginning, and it has this UPPER HAND self-evidently and without question. It is only we who must fight—and most of all against violence. So we must fight nonviolently.

But can we stand against violence using nonviolence and truly gain the UPPER HAND? Yes, but only if we already have the UPPER HAND—that is, if we trust fully and without reservation in the divine and only true UPPER HAND. Sometimes, the victory of nonviolence is revealed on a historical level, but admittedly not that often. The UPPER HAND, rather, points beyond time. In the words of the German Romantic poet, Friedrich Hölderlin: "What we are here"—and that includes all that we achieve on earth—"a God may there fulfill." And that God not only has the upper hand, but is the UPPER HAND.

Do the following lines from Rainer Maria Rilke's poem "Fall," in which the UPPER HAND catches us all, resonate with you?

> *We all must fall. This hand falls there.*
> *And look at others: It is in us all.*
> *And yet there's One who holds this fall*
> *in both his hands with infinite, tender care.*[5]

16 al-Wahhaab
the Giver and Lender, the SELF-GIVER

Some names of God express what we feel in the face of an encounter with the Great Mystery. One such example might be the Transcendent. Other names, however, spring from our contemplations of God. One such name is the SELF-GIVER. With the word God, we are pointing to the Ultimate Reality. But this reality is all-encompassing, so how could the all-encompassing Reality give us a gift that is limited? God, then, always gives Himself: unstintingly, wholly, and completely.

It is only the capacity of the vessels into which God pours Himself that is limited. And these "vessels" exist only because God, in the words of the Hassidic tradition, "took a step back" in order to allow space for the creation. Only by donating

Himself—that is, going outside Himself—can it even be possible for there to exist anything "outside of God." And giving God names is possible only because the SELF-GIVER shows us how he goes outside Himself. There is no name that could reach into the innermost nature of the Ultimate Reality. All there is, including ourselves, is an expression of this innermost nature and a site of encounter with the SELF-GIVER.

Can you remember the eyes from which a loved one's soul shone out to you, giving itself to you as a gift? The name of the SELF-GIVER points to a similar but infinitely larger self-giving donation.

17 ar-Razzaaq
the SUSTAINER, the Provider

Whenever we are inclined to worry, we should pray to the SUSTAINER. After all, we are never really self-sustaining. But nor are we ever unsustained, and we need only to reflect on our lives to realize this with amazing clarity. The mystic and poet Kabir describes the SUSTAINER as the one who "gave you radiance in your mother's womb," and goes on to ask: "Would such a one now let you walk around orphaned?" Those who call God the SUSTAINER trust in the fact that life will give them exactly what they need in that moment. And it requires only a little life experience to trust in this fact with conviction. Or do we really believe that we know best what we need? The German poet, Matthias Claudius, expresses this trust in the SUSTAINER succinctly:

God give me only every day,
such as I can, to live in.
Why should he give not so to me
what's to the sparrow given?[6]

Do you know anybody who worries about how to make ends meet? How can you help this person experience God's care today? Aren't all of us meant to be the eyes and hands of the SUSTAINER?

18 al-Fattaah
the OPENER

Our understanding of this name of God begins with wonder at the fact that there is space, that we have room for movement. Even when we say "being," we already mean not only the fullness of all there is, but the state of "being in flux," that is being. Being could instead be fixed, frozen in itself. And yet, everywhere around us and even within us, there is space—breathing space. Openness is part of the nature of reality as we experience it. And this openness is a gift.

That is why we call the divine wellspring from which this gift of openness flows to us the OPENER. How can we show our gratitude for the OPENER's gifts? By confidently daring to enter into this openness, breathing in deeply, breathing out deeply, and walking onward toward surprise. The OPENER is the God of surprise. Only because everything is open is there room for us to be surprised—and so the OPENER is also the God of hope. The OPENER allows us to experience hope as our own trusting openness to surprises.

A practical exercise: Open a door. Now remember all the doors that life has opened up to you, starting from when you were born. Take a deep breath, and as you breathe out, gratefully say the name of the OPENER.

19 al-'Aleem
the ALL-COMPREHENDING, the All-Knowing

How did human beings arrive at the idea that God is "all-knowing"? We may not know each step of this idea's historical development, but we can follow the internal logic: "God" stands for the Ultimate Reality we can experience, the kind we become conscious of in peak experiences, as we experience a "Now" that goes beyond the bounds of time. If this Ultimate Reality has consciousness—and if it did not, from where should we have consciousness?—this consciousness must contain all that is given. This has nothing to do with "fore-knowledge": there is no before and after in the eternal Now. Therefore, this consciousness does not diminish our freedom, which belongs to the realm of time.

All too often, the idea of the all-knowing God was misused as a threat. Even today, the idea makes some people think of a super-policeman who has everything under heavenly surveillance. So let us instead call God the ALL-COMPREHENDING, and thus shift the emphasis to God's compassionate understanding of our deepest motives. Such an insightful and therefore forgiving divine Thou is what our heart longs for—and that wish may find fulfillment in the ALL-COMPREHENDING.

Human beings have an insatiable wish to see and understand. But our longing to be seen and understood as who we really are goes even deeper. Think of an aspect of your life that, however much you try, you can't make clear to your most compassionate and understanding friend. And then lift your eyes to the ALL-COMPREHENDING.

20 al-Qaabiḍ
the WITHHOLDER

How often do we feel that fate is denying us something we have longed for? But who sends us that fate? Because we trust faithfully that the divine Mystery is the source and wellspring of our life, and therefore also of our fate, we ascribe this denial to God and call God the WITHHOLDER.

And yet, how often do we later realize how much good it did us that those things we hoped and prayed for were withheld? We are grateful to our parents not only for what they allowed, but also for all the things that they—through their greater and more mature insight—withheld from or denied us. Only as mature people can we fully appreciate what we owe our parents through their denial and withholding. And so gratefulness resonates within us when we speak the name of the WITHHOLDER.

Think back to something you wanted deeply but didn't get. It isn't too late to thank the WITHHOLDER for it. Maybe you can do so today and feel the inner freedom you get from gratefulness for what has been withheld.

21 al-Baasiṭ
the GRANTER, who grants gifts generously and abundantly

Everything is a gift—for there might instead have been nothing. This allows us to call the great "There" in the phrase "everything there is" the GRANTER, and also to imagine the joy of the one who opens His hand and fills all that lives with blessing. And for us too, "it is more blessed to give than to receive" (Acts 20:35).

But is that not simply a projection of human feelings onto God? One could answer with another question: From where should human beings have such feelings if they weren't "there"? They are given. And how could God give us something that God does not have? The joy we feel when we are able to grant others a wish is the joy of the GRANTER, manifesting in us. Furthermore, God is the act of granting itself, is the gift that gives all there is. In God, being and doing are one. And even though what we call God is infinitely greater than what we can grasp, we can experience God as the GRANTER, even within ourselves.

Can you think of anybody whose wish you can grant today? Who wouldn't want to receive a warm smile? That can be your opportunity to discover the GRANTER through your own act of granting.

22 al-Khaafiḍh
the REDUCER; the Giver of Humility, who brings low the arrogant and unjustly proud

We should remind ourselves that this name, like all the names of God, is trying to say something not just about what God does, but about who God is. In God, being and doing are one. The REDUCER who gives humility is Himself this humility. God is always giving Himself, even if our heart can take in no more of His abundance than our lungs can take in of all the air in the world. As the REDUCER, God is giving us a double gift of humility: the opportunity to turn our place in life into something that serves the good of others, and also the courage to do so.

Humility takes up this opportunity; it is the "courage to serve." Arrogant high-mindedness, however, seeks to receive service, compares and envies, tries to lift itself above others. In the end, it may drape itself in medals and honors, but it remains ridiculous. All those who are not humbly grateful for their place in life are brought low by life—but that too is a gift. Those who seek a place of superiority are shown their deserved place by life, which is to say by God the REDUCER. But every place is a place of honor. Those who recognize this can gratefully recognize the God as the Giver of Humility.

Where is your life offering you the best opportunity to serve others? That is where you can show the courage to serve today and discover the joy that humility gives us. And do not forget that, where necessary, receiving service can also be a courageous service.

23 ar-Raafi'
the UPLIFTER,
the Exalter of the Lowly and Humble

Somehow, we sense that not only humility is a divine gift, but all the life-affirming qualities of pride, too, come from God. Perhaps that is the reason for the term "high-mindedness." This high-mindedness has something to do with the feeling of exaltation when we stand on a high mountaintop, or when we feel "on top of the world" in some other place. Because we experience this exalted mood as a gift of being, we trace it back to God, whom we therefore call the UPLIFTER. Without God's grace, could we ever be uplifted so far beyond our everyday mindset?

The crucial difference between such a state and pride is probably the awareness that this inner exaltation is pure gift. Arrogant high-mindedness ascribes such uplift to itself, rather than to the UPLIFTER. But true awareness of our exaltation is not concerned with our social position or clout, but rather with a positive kind of pride, a pride without any kind of overbearing comparison with others. The image of such pride might be a stallion, rearing up with its mane blowing in the wind—an "earthen pride," as the poet says, a humble pride.

Consider for a moment that when you were conceived, you were just a microscopic cell, a thousand times smaller than a speck of dust. How did you become the being that now can read and contemplate these lines? With grateful awe, call the power of life that lifted you up above the dust the UPLIFTER.

24 al-Mu'izz
the HONORER,
the Bestower of True Honor

Honors we receive over the course of our life are quite fleeting. They disperse quickly; a little renown, and then we are forgotten. The recognition we receive from human beings will, after all, always remain a borrowed gift, sometimes borrowed all too briefly. But those who let themselves be taken up by that mysterious power which raises us beyond ourselves again and again—not from outside but from within—find that it not only uplifts but honors them, with an honor that is not merely a gift but a kind of inheritance into which we are born.

In the end, are we not clay, which some unfathomable dynamic honored with life, consciousness, self-confidence, and indeed, with the highest honor of a conscious relationship with the Great Mystery? For this reason, we dare to call the divine wellspring from which that dynamic arises the HONORER. The lasting honor which we human beings are given as a gift is the awareness of our intimate relationship with this power which honors us. In his poem "To the Unknown

God," the German philosopher Friedrich Nietzsche calls the addressee of the poem "ungraspable, familially my own." This awareness of being in relation to the ungraspable, of being matter raised to the conscious experience of God, is the incomparable honor for which we thank the HONORER.

The last verse of Friedrich Nietzsche's poem "To the Unknown God" is worth reflecting on closely. That verse fits with all the things the name of the HONORER is trying to tell us. It fits just as well with the previous and following names, the Uplifter and the Dishonorer:

> *I want to know you, You Unknown*
> *Who reach so deep into my soul,*
> *Who through my life like tempest roll,*
> *Ungraspable, familially my own.*
> *I want to know you, myself serve you.*[7]

25 al-Muzil
the DISHONORER, the Humiliator

Nicholas of Cusa refers to the Great Mystery as the *coincidentia oppositorum*: the coinciding of all opposites. For this reason, we can call God both the Honorer and the DISHONORER. How should we conceive of God dishonoring us? The answer must come from the same lived reality that lets us experience the honor done to us by God as the Honorer. Divine names are not like clothes that we place on an already familiar God as on a mannequin. No. Any God we can imagine is a graven image.

God's names spring from our glimpsed experiences of an unimaginable Ultimate Reality—and to us that vision is and always will be contradictory. By glimpsing a mere suspicion of its beauty, we become aware of two things simultaneously. On the one hand, it uplifts and honors us to admire such beauty, for looking at beauty transforms us and makes us more beautiful ourselves. On the other hand, we become aware that the overwhelming beauty we are touching practically destroys us. The German poet Rainer Maria Rilke knows this when he writes:

For beauty is nothing
but the beginning of the terrible
which we only just bear
and admire so deeply
because it casually disdains
to destroy us.[8]

Here is the paradox: the more deeply we glimpse God, the greater and yet more vanishingly insignificant we become. In this way, the Honorer becomes the DISHONORER, and vice versa.

Rainer Maria Rilke, who wrote those lines about beauty, also prays: "You are so great that I no longer am / When I approach proximity with you."[9] Think back to an experience of transcendent beauty. Didn't you feel that its beauty was uplifting you to the highest honor precisely because in your insignificance you "no longer were"?

26 as-Samee'
the ALL-HEARING ONE

God's names—which we should perhaps think of more as clues to God—point to an Ultimate Reality that is forever in-expressible. What can be said must remain on this side of the inexpressible, and so any name of God lies on our side of the relationship between God and us. And yet, those names say something not only about us, but about God, as well. The little ladybug that lands on my finger has a true experience of me, however limited that experience may be. If it could be put into words, the ladybug would say something about me that was true.

What we say of God is infinitely more insufficient, but it can nevertheless be true. This, for example, is the case when we call God the ALL-HEARING ONE: "When I call to You, You hear me." Anyone who wants to experience this must call out trustingly. Admittedly, the "answer" consists mainly of the awareness of having been heard. But is all that not mere projection? Yes, to the extent that every image is projection; no, to the extent that the image nevertheless captures something of reality. Listening to one another is a part of every real relationship, and so of our relationship with God, as well.

Can you think of anybody who seems alone even when they are surrounded by people? Maybe today you can make a point of listening attentively to that person. The ALL-HEARING ONE often listens through human ears.

27 al-Baṣeer
the ALL-SEEING ONE

Psychological research has confirmed that in moments of highest "mystical" awareness, we see differently than we usually do—with different eyes, one could say. In a sense, we then see things and people without reference to ourselves, but "as they are in themselves." In those moments, everything we see seems to us transfigured, radiant with an inner, sacred beauty.

When we are in love, we often spontaneously gaze at one another in this way. And we become aware that this way of looking shows us reality more truthfully than does a view jaded by daily habit. We no longer need to imagine that this is how God sees; we know, for in that moment, the Ultimate Reality is seeing through our eyes.

Those who call God the ALL-SEEING ONE are not merely saying that God sees, but are talking about how God sees. This can be comforting, particularly to those of us whose opinion of ourselves is low. The British writer C. S. Lewis once said that if human beings could see our beauty undisguised, we would fall down before one another as before gods. The ALL-SEEING ONE sees us in all our beauty.

Can you just look into a mirror, without making any kind of judgment about what you see? Look at yourself patiently, even lovingly, the way the ALL-SEEING ONE sees, the way a mother sees her child. Take your time and see if you can be "well pleased" with what you see.

28 al-Ḥakam
the JUDGE

When we speak or hear the name of the JUDGE, it takes effort not to imagine God as judgmental. In a world so estranged from God as ours, judging and judgment are poisoned, just as our idea of justice has been poisoned to its roots by retribution and revenge. To name God a "judge" after the judges familiar to us would be utterly mistaken. Such an image takes human ideas of justice at face value without questioning them. If, instead, we base our naming of God on our experience of God—as we should—we arrive at the name of the JUDGE because we experience the Ultimate Reality as ultimately justifying, that is, orienting us in a direction. And when we adjust ourselves to that direction, we realize how unjustified our so-called "justice system" actually is; its criminal justice consists, in the end, of a socially legitimized form of revenge. And it is precisely this kind of "justice" that God judges harshly. The judgment of God as the JUDGE is always mercy and forgiveness.

But how do we actually know that God, as the JUDGE, does not judge us with a view to revenge, but forgives and makes good? Can we be so sure? Yes, we know with the deepest certainty. Our most reliable convictions stem from the encounter with the Great Mystery, in the experience of universal oneness. And that is exactly where we find the root of an ethics that connects all of us, and of its guiding principle: "Do unto others as you would have them do unto you." Any morality must orient itself based on—that is, adjust itself to—this principle, just as every name of God must be interpreted in the light of our experience of God.

Reflect on some big injustice you have suffered or that you know from history. Can you imagine ways how justice might be restored? Think about this question until you have overcome every last bit of revenge. Gandhi was quite right to say that "an eye for an eye" will only make the whole world blind.

29 al-'Adl
the JUST

As children in school, our religion teacher made us memorize the sentence: "God is just. He rewards the good and punishes the wicked." That may not have been entirely wrong—but it is badly put and misleading. Above all, the very approach is wrong. One must not begin to know God through the third person singular, as if "He" were out there somewhere, a known quantity about which we now say something more. One can only begin with one's personal experience.

Everything we say about God testifies primarily to our human experience of God, and only indirectly to the Ultimate Reality. Divine names speak to our experience of that which is infinitely greater than anything that can be imagined. And so the name "the JUST" springs from our experience that the world has an orientation. It is working toward something, in a direction we can sense and, in turn, adjust ourselves to. Anything and everything that resists what reality is trying to realize must fail.

Our practical experience of reality teaches us this and allows us to say the same of the Ultimate Reality. Those who do not adjust themselves to justice are already judged—in this case, in the sense of condemned to fail. But those who earnestly strive for justice are justified by the JUST.

For example, gravity is one of reality's givens. We have to adjust ourselves to it. Once we do, we can build bridges and space-ships, and some of us can even walk a tightrope. But if we pre-tend there is no gravity, we will fall on our face with our very first step. What applies to gravity in the realm of physics ap-plies to the JUST in the realm of ethics.

30 al-Lateef
the SENSITIVE,
the Most Gentle, the Subtle One

Can we truly call God SENSITIVE and, therefore, ascribe feelings to God? We can answer this question with Yes. From where could we have feelings if the Ultimate Reality, to which we point with the word, "God," did not have them? God feels—at the very least in us. But it is not just within us that we can feel this tender sensitivity which makes us good. When we look closely around us, as well as outside of us, we can discover something akin to sensitivity. There is incredible subtlety in how, from the sub-atomic to the cosmic, the physical constants of interplay are interdependent and related. They create an order that can be expressed mathematically, brings forth life, and enables consciousness that can marvel with awe at such harmony.

Unfortunately, this aspect of the SENSITIVE has all too often been portrayed as a kind of cosmic piano tuner. We do not need this projection. The *whole*'s sensitivity to the *whole* is enough to make us kneel reverently. In and of itself, it is the holy presence in which—as in any human encounter—we are faced with infinitely more than time and space can encompass. Our personal encounter with this cosmic harmony allows us to address God as the SENSITIVE.

Whenever we feel that the world is cold and long for goodness, we can remember the tenderness and patience with which swallows feed their young. Would the all-pervading cosmic care of the SENSITIVE really stop short before it reaches us?

31 al-Khabeer
the INSIGHTFUL, the Knower
of the Impulses of the Heart

We arrive at the name of the INSIGHTFUL by following the train of thought that led us from the Judge to the Just to the Sensitive. Or should we say to the "Empathetic"? Here too, we are not starting from an unfulfilled longing which we then fashion a god to fulfill. Our starting point is sober, but deeply contemplated, inner and outer experience.

First, we observe the mathematical rules that give the entire cosmos order, direction, and coherence. Then, we consider that our consciousness is part of this cosmos, its interior view, as it were. Its key components are Self-consciousness and Thou-relation. From within us, we therefore know that the universe has a personal component. That is why we can speak not only of fine-tuned harmony but of sensitivity—and insight is the intellectual side of sensitivity to the subtle. For this reason, God, whose reality we encounter in all that is not eternal—though His Reality is infinitely greater than all that is finite—is truly the INSIGHTFUL.

Where do you feel misunderstood? You can hold up your innermost impulses, even those which are only just germinating and which you yourself hardly understand, to the loving gaze of the INSIGHTFUL, like buds up to the sunlight. God's loving insight will bring them to bloom.

32 al-Ḥaleem
The MOST FORBEARING, the Empathetic

Once again, the previous names of God leap forward to a new one: the Sensitive and Insightful must also be the MOST FORBEARING, who forgives all injustice. Because understanding means to enter fully, through sensitive empathy and insight, into that which is to be understood—actually to stand within it. And "to understand all is to forgive all." All that is unforgiven, all that seems unforgivable is, at its deepest level, simply that which we do not yet fully understand. Because all names of God point to the great Thou who is closer to us than we are to ourselves, who understands us intimately, it makes sense to call this understanding, forgiving Thou the MOST FORBEARING. Those who call God by this name and can earnestly mean it will, in the words of St. Benedict, "never despair of God's mercy."

To human beings, the reality we can experience is not, in the end, impersonal. Its beating heart is our innermost relation to a Thou that even makes it possible for us to say "I." However objective the scientific observations made by such an "I" may seem, they still depend on this Thou. And to whom do you tell your innermost stories, the ones nobody else understands? This understanding Thou is also a forgiving one. Maybe today, in gratefulness for the forbearance of the MOST FORBEARING, you can offer another person forbearance? Or maybe even yourself?

33 al-'Aẓeem
the SUBLIME,
the Supreme, the Magnificent

The meaning of sublimity and magnificence is brought home
to us in those moments psychology refers to as peak experiences. Peak experiences can be caused by a sublime sensuous
experience, like watching a waterfall or the rolling sea, or listening to a Beethoven symphony. But the sublimity we become conscious of during peak experiences is infinitely
beyond anything our senses can fully grasp. We therefore ascribe it to the Ultimate Reality and call God the SUBLIME. This
name, then, is linked to experiences in which we feel, simultaneously, our own smallness and something like godliness—
a sense that may be at the root of the biblical statement that
"God created humankind in his image, in the image of God
he created them" (Genesis 1:27). Psychological research has
found that the paradoxical feeling of being both vanishingly

small and boundlessly large at the same time is a character-istic of peak experiences. The name of the SUBLIME contains the same double quality: recognition of our nothingness and gratefulness for the overwhelming gift that God's magnificence has uplifted us above ourselves.

What do you find sublime in nature, in art, in human greatness? Does something of the SUBLIME shine through in those things? Does the encounter with sublimity lift you up above and beyond yourself? And, most importantly, does it give you an approach to life that also uplifts the others you encounter above and beyond themselves? If you open yourself up to that experience, you will see what the SUBLIME can do.

34 al-Ghafoor
the EVER-FORGIVING

The idea of "ever" presupposes time—but how can time fit into a name of God? Is not God's eternity the precise opposite of time? Yes, but all the names of God lie on our side, on the side of the world. Those things that belong to God's eternity are beyond what can be named. But time and eternity meet in a paradoxical way at the point of intersection—the Now. Now is ever occurring in time but is nevertheless the one, eternal "Now." Just as the light of the moon above the sea is mirrored in countless waves, rolling to shore again and again, repetition is eternal being, mirrored in time.

Since we know from experience that the Ultimate Reality is not impersonal and mechanical but, rather, at its core, is personal relationship, we can ascribe understanding and forgiveness to that Reality, calling God the All-Forgiving, indeed the EVER-FORGIVING. When we consciously return to the Now from the past and future concerns in which we are mired, we ever return to the realm of God's timeless forgiveness. Just as in the Middle Ages those fleeing punishment could seek sanctuary in a church, we can seek sanctuary in the Now.

What helps you keep finding your center in the Now? This centering is the purpose of any spiritual practice, such as grateful living. We can be grateful only now. The next time you are grateful, remember: you are standing in the Now, where forgiveness occurs—and ever recurs.

35 ash-Shakoor
the MOST GRATEFUL

Gratefulness has three parts: the act of giving, the gift, and
that joy of receiving, which we call thanks. All that there is
can be considered through these three aspects. The existence
of anything at all cannot be more deeply explained than that
it is a given—which is to say, that it sprang from giving. As
the word suggests, then, any given is a gift. Being is a gift
freely given to all that there is. And so the joy of being, as
such, is already the joy of receiving, and therefore thanks.
From this point of view, gratefulness is the nature of the entire universe. Even those things in nature that are not alive
"give thanks" through their being. All that lives gives thanks
by living. And we human beings express our gratefulness by
going from thinking to thanking. Not merely with words, but
living gratefully and making something of every gift in life;
acting in gratefulness.

The following reflection can lead us to the name of the MOST
GRATEFUL: the implied giver in the phrase "all that is given"
is the foundation of being, the wellspring and source of everything. But this foundation is not an impersonal It, but that

fundamental Thou which we call God. God, as the hidden foundation of all, gives Himself away as giver and gift; God as the innermost Reality of all that is given is gift; God as the joy of being in the heart of every being is thanks. Such an understanding of God makes our relationship with God extraordinarily intimate and dynamic. We become conscious of being part of what Christian mysticism calls the "round dance of the triune God." In that dance, not only humanity, but all that is given has no other task than gratefulness—through and with and in God the MOST GRATEFUL.

Can you think of something for which you are grateful? For example, look at your hand: Where does it ultimately come from? Its origin lies in nothingness, realized as potential. And this realization is pure gift. All that you do with your hand is already an expression of gratefulness for having received it as a gift. The more deeply you grow aware of this, the more you take part in the dynamics of gratefulness, and the more you participate in the life of the MOST GRATEFUL.

36 al-'Alee
the MOST HIGH, the Exalted

In naming the Ultimate Reality, we are concerned with the outermost bounds of what we can suspect or sense—and with what lies beyond those bounds. So it is not that surprising that we keep trying to outdo our utmost superlatives. And so we call the divine Reality the MOST HIGH, trying to express that all we can say about it can always be heightened further. But height refers only to one direction, while we also want to refer to the deepest depths: to all the unrealized possibilities that still lie hidden within the bosom of the creator.

Even that which we have actually been given and can access goes beyond the bounds of what we can imagine—such as the fact that a thimbleful of garden soil contains as many tiny organisms as there are people on earth. Human beings move in a middle realm between the immense and the miniscule—both are beyond our ability to grasp, and both awaken our deepest wonder. But who could distinguish this wonder from prayer?

Prayerful wonder is an experience of deep fulfillment—almost as if we human beings were naturally built for this attitude. Today, maybe you can take another look at an image of something immense, such as galaxies in the cosmos, and allow yourself to savor fully and enjoy the mixture of wonder and prayer you experience.

37 al-Kabeer
the GREATEST ONE

"God, Thou art great!" exults the German poet Rainer Maria Rilke. But he is well aware that as the GREATEST ONE, God shows his greatness mostly in the small things. And so the poet tries to find images that might approach an indication of God's greatness: mountain peaks, conflagrations of fire, a sandstorm in the desert...

I would have painted you, not on the wall
but edge to edge on sky, covering all,
and shaped you, as a titan tall
had shaped you: as mountain, fiery squall,
or seed growing from desert sand to sprawl—

Only to suddenly interrupt himself with a dash and a weighty "or":

or

it might be: once I almost found you . . .
So far away are my friends
that I can hardly hear their laughter cresting;
And you, young bird, have fallen from your nesting,
with yellow talons on my hand are resting.
My heart, seeing your eyes, with pity rends.
(Too broad my hand, which you now tends.)
And with my finger I lift a drop from the well
And strain your eager lunge for it to hear,
And feel the beat in your heart and mine swell,
and both with fear.[10]

Have you ever, in a moment of spontaneous empathy, felt how
far-reaching God's nearness is? Maybe you began to sense that
the greatness of the GREATEST ONE shows itself most of all in
the ability to encounter us in the smallest detail.

38 al-Ḥafeeẓ
the PRESERVER, and All-Protecting

Turning to the Ultimate Reality as the PRESERVER can resonate with a deeply peaceful sense of security. But before we
can earnestly and honestly call God by this name, we must
first succeed in taking two mental steps or achieving two insights—perhaps even without thinking too deeply about
them. First, we need to become aware that the Ultimate Reality cannot be impersonal; otherwise, where would we get all
the positive aspects we experience as part of our personhood?
We are part of reality. And this is the source of our second insight: because memory is a central part of our personhood,
we may also ascribe it to that Ultimate Reality we call God.
And under this double precondition, we call God, who holds
us in memory, the PRESERVER.

We can imagine God's memory as incomparably true—rather than as prone to lapses, as ours is. As we age, we forget a great number of things. And yet, nothing is lost, since the PRESERVER holds all things in memory. As for all things that distress us, all those things which we might like to leave forgotten: we may trust that the PRESERVER not only preserves but keeps those memories—that is, keeps them from doing harm.

Do you have memories you wish you could get rid of? Entrust them to the PRESERVER. Do you have memories that are particularly precious to you? Entrust those, too, to the PRESERVER.

39 al-Muqeet
the NOURISHER, the Sustainer

As soon as we awaken spiritually, we are filled with wonder: I exist! What a wonderful—and wondrous—fact. Furthermore, not only has the Ultimate Reality brought me forth and given me life, it also gives me everything I need in order to live. This is why, filled with grateful wonder, I call that divine Ultimate Reality the NOURISHER. It is true that in a culture as widely shaped by masculinity as ours, the NOURISHER sounds male—but the images that resonate with ideas of nourishing and being fed are primarily maternal. This is yet another way in which the experience of the living God constantly calls into question our terms and preconceptions, correcting them where necessary.

After all, our experience of the divine life—the experience we gain even just by living consciously—nourishes us no less than physical food nourishes us. The more we feel wonder at the gift that enables us to experience God as the NOURISHER through physical food and drink, the more grateful we become. And the more grateful we become, the more deeply wakeful and alive we become, as well. By being nourished on the maternal breast of God, the NOURISHER, we grow—both inside and out.

Imagine a table piled with all the nourishment you consume in a week. If you want to imagine a month's nourishment, you will need a big table. But now imagine a year. And for how many years have you been nourished already? Where did all this nourishment come from? Think of all the teachers giving you food for thought. We nourish one another. The NOURISHER works in us and through us. Whom can you help nourish today? Find a specific person in answer to this question.

40 al-Ḥaseeb
the RECKONER, the One who Calculates or Takes Account

How wondrous it is that everything in the cosmos, from the unimaginably large to the unimaginably small, accords with an order that can be grasped mathematically! Our wonderment is probably also expressed by our calling God the RECKONER. Obviously, the word's conventional meaning of "unloving, cold, and self-serving" does not apply.

In the same way, the idea that the RECKONER takes account of things in the sense of chalking up our mistakes would be a dangerous distortion. But trusting that the RECKONER has ordered "all things by measure and number and weight" (Wisdom 11:21) can give us a deep confidence: we are counted and accounted for in the great order of all things, in an order that is infallibly precise, but never cold—because it springs from love.

Do you know the feeling of satisfaction that someone who isn't great at math experiences when a complicated calculation comes out right? We can feel something similar when we become aware that, although we cannot even count the hairs on our own head, we can trust that the RECKONER has weighed the "household budget" of the entire universe to the very last decimal place—and that behind this whimsical image hides overwhelming Reality.

41 al-Jaleel
The MAJESTIC ONE

When one of God's names resonates so clearly with political overtones, it should give us pause. The MAJESTIC ONE, after all, is not some vast projection of royal or imperial majesty onto God. Throughout the history of the world, earthly majesties have always had pretensions of being the earthly representatives of the MAJESTIC ONE—and a servile priestly caste has supported them in this project.

But those who call God the MAJESTIC ONE are thus challenging all other conceptions of majesty. The powerful cannot teach us how God acts; rather, God teaches the powerful how they should be acting. And this fundamental principle can be applied to the political situation of any historical era. There has hardly ever been a time when one could call God the MAJESTIC ONE in earnest without being seen by prevailing society as a rabble-rouser—and indeed being one. What does the MAJESTIC ONE actually demand of earthly majesties?

A saying ascribed to Jesus answers this question: "The greatest among you will be your servant" (Matthew 23:11). Whom can you serve today, and in what way? Imagine exactly how and where, and then actually commit to doing it. Carry out your plan, and you will discover a surprise waiting for you: you will not feel superior afterward, but truly noble, truly majestic—because it was the MAJESTIC ONE serving others through you and in you.

42 al-Kareem
the MOST GENEROUS, the Magnanimous

Majesty and generosity belong together. Small-mindedness that acts majestically is only making itself ridiculous. Wherever we look, reality proves to be not only majestic but also filled with bountiful generosity—indeed, almost wasteful. In the words of the Swiss pedagogue Johann Heinrich Pestalozzi: "Out of a thousand blossoms, barely one ripens into the fruit of autumn"—and out of millions of sperm cells, only one fertilizes the egg; out of countless possibilities, time and time again, only one is realized.

Is that not an almost lighthearted generosity? If the tangible reality before us is already so ostentatiously bountiful, why should we not then call the truth beyond all other truths the MOST GENEROUS? And regarding lighthearted generosity, the perceptive Austrian writer, Marie von Ebner-Eschenbach, smilingly opines: "If magnanimity is to be consummate, it must contain a quantum of lightheartedness." In all likelihood, she is right—and through this idea, the MOST GENEROUS may be leading us to discover God's lightheartedness. This discovery can save us when we are at risk of taking ourselves all too seriously.

When do you tend to take yourself too seriously? Think deeply about whether it isn't always linked to a certain small-mindedness. Remember: You are a child of the MOST GENEROUS. Today, let yourself do something that seems almost too lighthearted and irreverent. You may experience just how easy and exhilarated we are allowed to feel within ourselves.

43 ar-Raqeeb
the WAKEFUL, the Watchful

A legend states that, in a nightly vision, St. Benedict of Nursia saw the entire universe before him "as if encompassed in a single beam of sunlight." By way of explanation, his biographer Gregory the Great adds that Benedict, "in heavenly transports," had "beheld the narrowness of all earthly things."

It might have been comparable mystical experiences that led to God being named the WAKEFUL. If even we human beings can encompass the entire universe in an enraptured gaze, then by how much more can God? But there is another idea resonating in the name: the WAKEFUL not only sees but observes the seen with wakeful attention. In my childhood days, the sitting rooms of many faithful Christians contained images of the great eye of God watching over all things. I have to admit that those could sometimes even be somewhat frightening. But a wise teacher prevented me from falling into the misunderstanding that God wanted to spy on us from the sky. She told us: "God is not watching over your every step in order to catch you out in every mistake. No! God loves you so much that he can't take his eyes off you."

Do you love someone so much that you can't take your eyes off them? We call someone like that "dear to us" or "our treasure" in order to express how much we value them. So calling God the WAKEFUL should raise our self-esteem! And it should strengthen our reverence for the dignity of our fellow human beings that the WAKEFUL looks lovingly over them day and night.

44 al-Mujeeb
the RESPONSIVE ONE,
the Answerer of Prayers

All traditions that speak of God also speak with God. This presupposes trust in God as the All-Hearing One, indeed, as the RESPONSIVE ONE. Admittedly, not all prayers are pleas or requests. And why should such petitionary prayers occur more often in our conversation with God than pleas or requests occur in conversations with our fellow human beings? Undeniably, those who speak with God must also consequently assume that God hears prayers and, as a loving God, answers them.

This is a daring claim. It dares to affirm a worldview in which freedom has a place—not in the sense of God's freedom to intervene "externally" and "after the fact," but as the freedom of each individual part to grow, determined by and determining the cohesive whole. The idea of prayer as a dialogue with the great Thou at the heart of the Ultimate Reality effortlessly fits into such a worldview. So why should pleas and requests—petitionary prayer—not also be a part of such dialogue?

Admittedly, the RESPONSIVE ONE can also give very different kinds of answers to prayer, such as "No," "Not yet," or "Yes, but not in that way." All these are valid answers to prayer.

What do you ask the RESPONSIVE ONE for? Isn't every heartfelt wish, such as for a sick friend's recovery, a prayer of the heart, whether we call it that or not? And what are you expecting from it? What wishes do others have—even if they have never expressed them—that you could answer today in the name of the RESPONSIVE ONE? Think hard.

45 al-Waasi'
the ALL-ENCOMPASSING, the Boundless

The Ultimate Reality can exclude nothing. This reflection allows us to call God the ALL-ENCOMPASSING. But this naming involves far more than merely a logical conclusion. Such a divine name could only ever come from a mystical insight, which goes beyond logic but without contradicting it. The ALL-ENCOMPASSING must, for example, encompass Non-Being as well as Being, No as well as Yes, Evil as well as Good. The word, "encompass," resonates with the full dynamic of affirming, giving meaning, connecting, surrounding, and indeed, embracing. This dynamic does not deny the inherent contradictions but overcomes them at a higher level.

Once again, we can see how a divine name affects those who speak it in faith: only those who are willing to be made ever more encompassing by the ALL-ENCOMPASSING may dare to call God by this name. The life we live is divine life, and the breath we breathe is the spirit of God within us. And so, from within us, the ALL-ENCOMPASSING will allow us to embrace ever-greater contradictions.

Where do you draw boundaries? Who or what do you exclude? What would it cost you to embrace even those outside your boundaries in the way the ALL-ENCOMPASSING embraces them? Doing so doesn't necessarily require approving of them. Only you can know what it might cost you—but what you stand to gain is nothing less than true fullness of life.

46 al-Ḥakeem
the ALL-WISE

Perhaps the essence of wisdom is that, unlike knowledge, it encompasses and affirms paradoxical contradictions. Given this idea alone, it is only a single step from calling God the All-Encompassing to calling God the ALL-WISE. When we think of wisdom, we initially think of a human characteristic, as did the medieval mystic Bernard of Clairvaux, when he said: "To grasp a thing brings a man knowledge; to be touched by a thing makes him wise."

But we should not forget that human wisdom is granted to us in those moments when we let ourselves be touched by divine wisdom. Our peak experiences are moments of being deeply touched. These significant experiences that we have been given must not be wasted. We can keep calling them to memory, these moments in which our heart transcended the boundaries of reason and spontaneously spoke an all-encompassing Yes. All that is missing, then, is for us to turn this Yes into a reality through all that we do and suffer. That act glorifies the ALL-WISE in our everyday life.

Saying Yes, or rather, living Yes in such a way requires courage and serenity. These two attitudes are tellingly linked with wisdom in the familiar prayer of Alcoholics Anonymous: "God grant me the serenity to accept the things I cannot change, the courage to change the things I can, and the wisdom to know the difference."

47 al-Wadood
the ALL-LOVING

Calling God all-encompassing already implies that it is God's love which encompasses all, but for our feelings it is important to clearly articulate this fact by calling God the ALL-LOVING—whose love encompasses all. It is important to keep reminding ourselves that love can be understood as a radical Yes to belonging. In the end, even thinking about reality leads us to two givens that cannot be themselves questioned: the "Yes," and the relation, "What is, is." That is to say, "Yes," and "everything hangs together with everything else"—in a word, relationship.

Any being—anything that is—becomes what it is only through its relationship to other things that are, and comes to belong to itself only through love, through this Yes. Anything we say about love resonates with all the joy and fullness of life we know from our human, loving relationships—and rightly so: our Yes to belonging finds its highest fulfillment in our living relationship with the ALL-LOVING, who encompasses all with His love.

Have you ever watched how every living thing thrives when loved? You can try it for yourself: on children best of all, but also on guinea pigs, or on cactuses. To me, the runner ducks in our monastery are a perfect example: they live on love—and, of course, on snails. What being can you help thrive today by encompassing it in the love of the ALL-LOVING—and thereby yourself become more fully alive?

48
the GLORIOUS, the Most Noble

One starting point for many of the different divine names is wonderment; another is gratefulness. Both of these feelings resonate in the name of the GLORIOUS. The more attentively we observe the world, the more worthy of wonderment become all those things that are given. And if I once again "switch lenses" and let my observation become encounter, then wonderment at what is given becomes augmented by gratefulness—gratefulness for the fact that everything that is given is truly a gift given to me.

Whenever this gratefulness makes my heart sing, then I bow down gratefully before the wellspring of all that is given, and I wonderingly praise all that it brings forth. But I too spring from this source, and my praise springs from it too. We are part of this abundance: it flows in us and through us, although it goes infinitely beyond us. It is the GLORIOUS who fills my eyes, heart, and mouth with glorification, for God is not only glorified, but glorifying. And there is nothing that could more intimately unify us with the GLORIOUS than grateful, wondering glorification.

Can you think of a thing, a living being, or a creation of the human mind that you truly admire? A landscape, a teacher, a poem? Today, take a moment simply to admire it first, and then let yourself become conscious of what a gift has been given to you. The feeling rising up in you as you become conscious of this gift is glory from the abundance of the GLORIOUS.

49 al-Baa'ith
the AWAKENER,
the Raiser of the Dead

To understand this divine name, we must enter into the realm of mythological ideas. But we will also return with insights that remain valid and helpful for our everyday life. In mythology, death is considered a form of sleep from which the AWAKENER will call us back to wakeful life on the "Day of Judgment," which refers to the day at the end of all days. A great deal of insight is clothed in this image: that God stands outside life and death, even outside time, in the eternal Now; and above all, that God wants to give us a part in timeless and, therefore, unending life. The awakening is a gentle image indicating that true aliveness begins with a wakeful relationship with God.

But why should we wait and awaken only on the last day? Even today, we can encounter the AWAKENER if we pause and become aware of the many things in our life that are outside time and, therefore, are everlasting. For example, any truly heartfelt relationship between human beings goes beyond time because it reaches into the eternal Mystery. The more consciously we dwell in that part of our life that transcends time, the more alive we become through the AWAKENER. Those who live only in time are already dead. The more we live our lives oriented toward God, the more we grow beyond the fading and temporal—yes, even now!

Close your eyes, take a deep breath, and become aware of how a mysterious reality that we call life is enlivening you. Now remember that the Great Mystery is not an impersonal, mechanical reality but your fundamental Thou—and already, the AWAKENER is giving you a brief taste of the bliss of fully wakeful life for which you are meant beyond time.

50 ash-Shaheed
the ALL-WITNESSING, the Witness

During the difficult illness that was soon to lead to her death, my mother once turned to me and said almost solemnly: "You see how I suffer." Only later—I had to mature through my own suffering first—did I realize what I had been experiencing with my mother. The most intense suffering plunges us into a feeling of utter forlornness. An unbridgeable chasm seems to separate us from normal life in the world of the healthy. We do not wish for someone else to suffer as we do, but we do long for someone to at least understand how hard our suffering is, to be a Witness. It is not about evidence but about empathy, not about testimony that confirms but about an ALL-WITNESSING who consoles.

Recall that those who use the word "God" are using it to point to the insight that the Ultimate Reality is not impersonal, but that we stand in a personal relationship to it and can cultivate this relationship. By calling God the ALL-WITNESSING, we are laying in that name all our trust that, based on our personal relationship with the foundation and wellspring of all reality, everything that is important to us, including the harrowing experience of forlornness, is honored, dignified, and preserved in the eternal Now.

Do you long for the gaze of somebody who cares about how you are doing? Maybe today somebody is longing for you to be such a witness? The ALL-WITNESSING often gazes out at us from human eyes and often only truly manifests through our fellow human beings.

51 al-Ḥaqq
the ABSOLUTE TRUTH

"What is truth?" Since time immemorial, philosophers have grappled with this question. At issue is not one particular truth or another, but truth in and of itself. As soon as we express an insight into truth, it becomes only a partial truth, for words and concepts can never grasp the entirety of truth. But the human heart longs for all-encompassing truth, and we can sense such truth only beyond words and concepts.

The word "God" points to an undoubtable reality—just like the "There" in the sentence, "There is a universe." Even those who deny God cannot deny this reality, since even when they say that "there is no God," there is, in the words of the American writer Gertrude Stein, a "there there." The sentence may cast doubt on the way a particular person imagines God. But nevertheless, the "there" is in that sentence, too. And understood correctly, this "there" points to the Great Mystery, from which everything is given. Everything springs from "there," and that Great Mystery is also called "God." It is all-encompassing, unimaginable, necessary for thought, not illogical, but beyond logic and beyond doubt. And given all these facets, God—or the "there"—is called the ABSOLUTE TRUTH.

Can I suggest a game that may help continue this train of thought? Just say to yourself: "There is ... (or are...)" and complete the sentence with the first thing to come into your head. Fireflies, heart transplants, conscientious-objector status. Then repeat the sentence to yourself and try to trace the connection between what came into your head and the "there" which is the source and wellspring of all things. Perhaps the thought will turn into more than reflection—perhaps even into a kind of awe before the Mystery.

52 al-Wakeel
the TRUSTWORTHY, the dependable Helper and Guardian, the Trustee

We must never forget that belief means a radical trust. So whoever believes in God already implicitly means the TRUSTWORTHY. When we speak this name, we are emphasizing that we trust God. At the same time, the name points to a significant distinction: the distinction between believing something, in the sense of considering something true, and belief in something, in the sense of trusting. When I believe something, then in the end I am trusting myself, trusting in my own cleverness and discernment.

But when I believe in someone, then I am relying on that person. What a radical statement! It means that I leave the realm of my own reasoned discernment and enter into a highly personal relationship of trust. My "I" is something that is always concerned with a *thing*; my "Self," however, is a person concerned with personal relation, and in the end, divine relation.

Personal relationships are always mutual. Calling God the TRUSTWORTHY presupposes that we give God trust. God, in turn, gives us the gift of trust in two ways: God does not disappoint our trust, which is the first great gift. Beyond that, however, God grants us free will and the space in which to exercise it. In so doing, God is giving us the gift of freedom and thus showing the utmost trust.

Think about your relationship with your friends. Which of the two halves of the gift of trust comes easier to you? Proving trustworthy—or trustingly offering space? This question can also be helpful in the relationship between parents and children.

53 al-Qawiyy
the STRONG ONE

No human being is capable of proving worthy of another's deepest trust. This is due not to faithlessness but to inconstancy, if not of our will then at least of our life itself, which is ever changing and bounded by death. This weakness of human trustworthiness lets us now call God—whom in contrast we know as the Steadfast, the Powerful, and the Trustworthy—the STRONG ONE.

Here we must once again remind ourselves that, in all of these divine names, it is not so much about fixed ideas of God, but about relationship: the relationship between my "I" and the divine "Thou." Here, then, it is about the relationship between my weakness and God as the STRONG ONE. With the German poet Johannes Scheffler, also known as Angelus Silesius, I can sing "I seek to love you, my strength!" And since love is the mutual affirmation of belonging, my belonging to the STRONG ONE fills me with a strength that overcomes all inconstancy with an eternally resounding Yes.

An eternal Yes? I am in time, so how could I give an eternal Yes? I can, if my "Self" speaks this Yes, not just my "I" alone. The Self lives in the Now, and the Now transcends time and reaches into eternity. The more I practice living consciously in the Now, the more my relationships will grow beyond the limits of time.

54 al-Mateen
the FIRM,
the ENDURING, the Steadfast

Rilke succinctly describes a fundamental aspect of the human condition:

> Tremulous, we long to find a hold;
> Too young, we sometimes long for what is old,
> too old, we long for things that never were.[11]

Longing for something to hold on to, we seek the truly FIRM, the ENDURING, but we cannot find it in a world in which all things flow, in which everything changes and decays, in the world of objects. And yet, we also have access to another world, or more precisely to a different dimension of the same world, to the world of the present. Our "I" lives as an object among objects, decaying along with all the objects around us. But our "Self" lives in the Now, in the present and presence of the "Thou," and this relationship endures beyond time. The more we cultivate our relationship with the great Thou toward which our Self at its innermost is oriented, the more clearly we can experience this Thou as the FIRM, the ENDURING, for which we long so deeply.

And how do we start living our everyday lives in reference to the Thou? Martin Buber advises us first to pay attention to the difference between impersonal use and personal relationship. Then we can keep making the "I-Thou" relationship, instead of "I-It" use, more and more our fundamental attitude. We can take this attitude even toward plants, animals, and things, because they can also cause us to encounter the great Thou. Today, spend a few quiet moments with something, long enough to sense the presence of the FIRM, the ENDURING in it.

55 al-Waliyy
the Shield, the Friend,
the PROTECTOR

To protect originally meant to cover something from in front—to stand between something and danger. In this sense, friends protect one another by shielding one another. But from what are we protected by that mysterious presence we call the Shield, the Friend, and the PROTECTOR? We trust that God protects us from all that might harm us.

And, we may further ask, does this Friend protect only His own friends, only those who rely on and trust in Him? Does a mother protect only those of her children who explicitly ask her to be protected? Surely not. So why should we imagine that God chooses who deserves protection and who does not? Even though we may consciously entrust ourselves to the PROTECTOR, this Friend already protects us from the very worst. And that act protects our friends from the worst as well—namely from loneliness, because they know that we stand by them and stand with them, even when we cannot prevent harm from coming to them.

There is an example that I experienced myself and remains un- forgettably in my memory: David Givens was popular with his school friends, even if they did sometimes good-naturedly rib him for living almost like a monk. He was never preachy, but something about his friends did change when he was among them. One Friday evening, David was in a car with a group of raucous friends when the car crashed into a tree. All survived, except David. In his trouser pocket, they found a quotation from the Bible, copied down in his handwriting: "No one has greater love than this, to lay down one's life for one's friends" (John 15:13). A friend can be a protector to us in so many and varied ways—and through us, to our friends.

56 al-Ḥameed
the PRAISEWORTHY,
to whom all Thanks accrue

"Praising, that's it!" With this call, like the sounding of a trumpet, the poet Rilke begins one of his poems and thus encapsulates the meaning and purpose of our human lives. Praise is the actual purpose of our life, and when we fulfill it, our life has meaning. Admittedly, "praising" in this context does not mean singing hymns of adoration. Instead, it means an existence heightened to the point of song—for, as Rilke says elsewhere, "Song is being."

And so a handful of soil in the garden praises existence just by being. A cabbage praises by growing, the caterpillar nibbling on it praises by feeding itself, and the girl walking up to it with the kitchen knife to harvest it is praising through her culinary prowess. Everything that exists is "praising" simply by being, by developing and fulfilling itself.

But whom or what are we praising through all that we think, do, and suffer in our life? The answer is: the whole. "Consider the whole: Praise the whole!" says St. Augustine. Only in grasping the whole can we recognize being as praiseworthy. And when we look at the heart of the whole with the eyes of the heart—that is, from the point of view of our innermost personal relationship—we can recognize the PRAISEWORTHY.

From your own experience, you know the difference between looking at something closely and looking at a person you are encountering eye to eye. Through this "I–Thou" mode of looking, anything you look at seems praiseworthy, from the tiniest flower to the all-encompassing whole of being. Which way of looking goes deeper? Which way do you want to trust in the end?

57 al-Muḥṣee
ALL-RECORDING

Numerous times in this list, we have encountered divine names pointing to a faithful witness for whom the human heart longs: the All-Comprehending, the All-Hearing One, the All-Seeing One, the Preserver, the Witness, and now the ALL-RECORDING. Behind all of these names stands the image of a conscientious biographer to whom everything, even the smallest personal detail, seems so significant that it is worth being recorded and immortalized.

All these names can be read as variations on the theme of the eternal "Thou" of which our human "I" becomes aware as soon as we grow into consciousness; that very "Thou" that makes it possible even for me to say "I" at all. This particular name resonates with the Book of Isaiah, where God tells us,

"See, I have inscribed you on the palms of my hands" (Isaiah 49:16). We are tattooed, engraved, lovingly written into the hands of the ALL-RECORDING. This divine name tells us that, to God, we are unforgettable.

Yes, that is what our heart longs for. But is it true, or just wishful thinking? We need to tackle this crucial question in every personal encounter that seems too good to be true. Every "you" is just a face of our fundamental "Thou" at the foundation of the Great Mystery. Can you open yourself to human love? If so, you have already decided that the ALL-RECORDING is true. Truth is made of one piece, and if we jump into it, we fall all the way to the foundations, no matter how deep we think they may be.

58 al-Mubdi'
the ALL-BEGINNING, the Initiator

At a certain age, children often ask tirelessly where things come from. When we began to think, we were all little philosophers, driven to philosophical questioning by one thing: wonderment. Plato knew that philosophy begins with wonderment, and as children, we were still capable of wondering at the fact that there exists something rather than nothing. In adulthood, most of us have unlearned this capacity for deep wonderment that lets children question where we come from, and indeed, where everything comes from. We must, then, relearn to ask, brimming with wonderment, the question of the origin of all things. But because our thinking has now become so entangled in past and future, we risk imagining the origin—the wellspring we are concerned with—as some point in the past, perhaps as the Big Bang. We must proceed more radically, asking where time itself has its origins, which is in the Now. This time-transcending Reality, diving headlong into time, is what we mean when we speak of the ALL-BEGINNING.

Think back to something you experienced in the past. However far back it may be, doesn't memory bring it back to the Now? And when the future comes, it will come as Now. You can't find it on the face of a clock, this Now, in which we have our being. Rilke says:

> For with their minute steps, the clocks
> Go side-by-side with our actual day.[12]

If you can immerse yourself in the endlessly quiet Now, next to which the tick-tocking of the clocks is tiptoeing, you can sense the ALL-BEGINNING. When were you last filled with wonder at the Now? Where can you find something today to wonder at?

59 al-Mu'eed
the All-REPEATING, the Restorer

We arrive at this divine name when we take the previous name as our starting point but alter our perspective. We can encounter the All-Beginning only in the timeless Now, for that is what gives time its beginning. We have access to this Now because it is where our Self lives. Our "I," however, lives in time, and so we can observe the All-Beginning from a temporal perspective as the ALL-REPEATING.

Repetition is the eternal mirrored in time. Another image of one mirrored in many might also be the moon, reflected in countless drops of water. Just as we can see our being as a gift of the All-Beginning, the ALL-REPEATING gives us the possibility of change, growth, and fulfillment. That is also how we may imagine time: the eternal present is so inexhaustibly full of possibility that the ALL-REPEATING is offering us new opportunities in every instant. Each moment, then, is a mysterious intersection between beginning and repetition, between eternity and time.

Every moment is in the eternal Now, but also in time. So every moment gives us the opportunity for a fresh start. This is the gift of the ALL-REPEATING. Are you ready to show your gratefulness by taking that opportunity? And where can you make a fresh start today?

60 al-Muḥyee
the GIVER OF LIFE

Every instant gives us the opportunity for a fresh start: a beginning of new aliveness. And this aliveness is expressed by realizing relationships. Before we can speak of life in its true sense, a being must have three relationships, which we know from our own experience as living beings.

1. The relationship of actual existence to the mere potentiality of being. We share this relationship with non-living beings: we exist—we are "a given," and this "giving," together with the perception of being given, constitutes a deep, fundamental relationship.

2. The relationship between inner and outer. On a purely physical level, it is a feature of even the simplest living beings that they have an interior that defines their exterior and interacts with it. At all further levels, aliveness is realized through ever more complex forms of this interaction between give and take.

3. The relationship between a given and the still potential. This third relationship creates a space for growth and development.

And so, as my aliveness occurs in the form of a constant give and take, I may call this unfathomable "Thou-I" encounter in these relationships the GIVER OF LIFE.

Does this sound dry and philosophical? Maybe. But if we live our life by it, it makes the huge difference between merely going through the motions of life and the adventure of the deepest relationship open to us human beings: our relationship with the GIVER OF LIFE. As a human being, the more personally I take my relationship, the more alive I become. That includes the relationships with the mystery of my origins, with my surroundings and fellow beings, and, by transcending myself, with my own still unrealized possibilities.

61 al-Mumeet
the BRINGER OF DEATH, in whose Hand is Death

Life and death are inseparably linked. It is for this reason that the Giver of Life is also the BRINGER OF DEATH. The two names point to two polar aspects of one and the same incontrovertible truth. Both aspects must be kept in mind: first, because only in this way can we live wakefully and joyfully; and second, because doing so teaches us how to die with trust. Only those who say Yes to death are also saying a full Yes to life—if only because we must let go fully in each moment in order to savor the next to the fullest extent. And this act of letting go is dying to the past in order to live fully in the Now. And if we do not let go, some part of us is clinging to the past, and we will be split and living half a life.

The more we practice letting go, the more easily we will be able to live—and the more easily we will be able to die. Death may remain a mystery to us, but all that we need in order to prepare ourselves well can be learned from our daily experience: when we let go before we fall asleep and die to the day we have lived through, we will awaken the next day lighter and more joyful. Should not such an exercise also make it easier to let go in our last hour, full of trust?

Admittedly, trusting the BRINGER OF DEATH sounds strange. But life and death are givens and they can't be denied. We have a choice: either we can go up against givens or we can receive them trustingly and gratefully as gifts. Going up against them is not only useless, it also makes death and even the life before it painful. All the gifts of the Giver of Life sooner or later prove to be good gifts. The same has to be true of the gifts of the BRINGER OF DEATH, because both are names for one and the same Ultimate Reality unfathomable to us.

62 al-Ḥayy
the EVER-LIVING

Again and again, the 99 names of God resonate with wonder at the mystery of life. This is hardly surprising, since the name, "God," points to our encounter with what we cannot fathom. And what could be a more unfathomable mystery to us than life itself? The names refract this unfathomable mystery into its manifold aspects, just as a prism refracts a single sunbeam into many hues.

The encounter with this unfathomable mystery is a gift. It occurs and is fulfilled within us but remains beyond our grasp, since the grasp of our reason is itself only an aspect of our aliveness, just like our embodiment, our senses, or our will. Other divine names, such as the Giver of Life, spring from our experience of the gift of life. When we, as living human beings, call God the EVER-LIVING, we are feeling our way in wondering toward the gift, which is that we may partake of an aliveness that extends infinitely beyond what we can imagine.

The apostle Paul is said to have agreed with the words of a Greek poet that in God "we live and move and have our being" (Acts 17:28). Does such an intimate relationship with God feel presumptuous to you? Take a deep breath. Feel how alive you are. Let yourself wonder reverently at the mysterious power working in you and also infinitely beyond you. That is what is meant by the EVER-LIVING.

63 al-Qayyoom
the ETERNAL

We live in time, but we also know something that we call infinity—the counterpoint to time. Eternity remains, time runs
out. While time may be a gift, allowing us as it does to start
fresh over and over again and offering us one opportunity
after another, we nevertheless long for eternity. Amid tran-
sience, we long for permanence. We are also familiar with
the Now as the intersection of time and eternity. And we
know, because in the Now we take part in a truth that is not
subject to time, that our existence transcends time.

There are many moments, but only one Now to which each
moment affords us access. The countless moments are like
gates, all of which lead to freedom, to the one Now. Encounter

takes place at each of these gates where true communion occurs. They not only open up to us a view into a dimension beyond time, but also let in light, giving even our temporality's most meager trappings a shimmer of eternity. We must dare to approach these gates to the Now if we are truly to sense that power which we personify as the ETERNAL.

We experience time as growth and decay, but the Now as fulfilled reality. I can't stop my decay in time, but I can counter it with Self-fulfillment in the Now. Every spiritual practice aims to serve this purpose by leading to the Now and to an encounter with the ETERNAL. In your everyday life, what is your most effortless path to the Now?

64 al-Waajid
the GIVER OF BEING

When we name that Ultimate Reality to which we as human beings are oriented, two things occur: we become consciously aware of a Higher Power in our lives and we open ourselves up to a personal relationship with that power by addressing it by name.

The first of these two steps is self-explanatory. The Higher Power, here, is clearly evident: as soon as we begin to consider the fundamental force in the universe to which we owe our being, we realize that it must be at least as real as all that it effects. If we then look not only with the gaze of insight but also with the gaze of encounter—as we must whenever we want to see reality as a whole—we become conscious of this Higher Power as that mysterious "Thou" which we call God. We address it by name, not because we are personifying it through our imagination but because we recognize that the very existence of our imagination and personhood is owed to that Power. And by opening ourselves up to the personal nature of this Higher Power, we encounter that "Thou" which enables us to perceive ourselves as "I."

In the connection of these two modes of experience—insight and encounter—this clearly discernible Higher Power becomes the GIVER OF BEING whom we may personally encounter.

Why is it important to look not only as we do for insight but also as we do in relationship? Because when we do, mere thinking becomes thanking. And gratefulness is the key to a joyful life. Do you want to experiment with this idea? Try, for example, to let a coin drop to the ground, roll, and settle. Science can tell us much about gravity, but in the end, it remains an unexplainable given, one of the forces in the harmonious ensemble that support our being. Even wonderment at this support ennobles you. But gratefulness for this support through the GIVER OF BEING can always keep bringing you joy—a joy you can pass on!

65 al-Maajid
the RESPLENDENT, the Magnificent

On the surface, a number of divine names sound to us like honorary titles that potentates like to give themselves. One of those is the RESPLENDENT. But we must probe this more deeply. The names of God express insights familiar to us from our inner experience, or those we have gained from encounters with creation. We call the RESPLENDENT by this name because nature in its beauty seems to us gloriously resplendent. In a sense, beauty might be the more obvious term—but it is radiant beauty we mean when we say "resplendent," and we should always be conscious of that aspect when we speak of God as the RESPLENDENT.

Why is this important? Because God's goodness and truth are frequently invoked, while God's beauty is all too often neglected. This means that our senses are given short shrift. Goodness draws on the will, truth satisfies our reason, but beauty speaks to our senses and exalts them all. Compared with all else, this makes beauty into that proverbial one drop of honey with which you catch more flies than with vinegar. The RESPLENDENT—the Magnificent—is a God who can thrill the imagination.

Today, take some time to look at, listen to, smell, taste, or feel something truly beautiful. When you plan to make that time, also plan to consciously open yourself up to the RESPLENDENT.

66 al-Waaḥid
the ONE

O fountainhead, providing, Thou mouth
which bottomlessly speaks but one pure thing.[13]

Thus Rilke reacts to one of the ancient fountains from whose masks' mouths an uninterrupted stream of water has been flowing into the marble basin below—sometimes for centuries. But he seems to see more behind this image than is initially apparent. Just the tone of the language and the solemn address say as much. In fact, that address is actually directed far beyond the fountain, at the fount and wellspring of all reality.

This is how deeply the poet is listening, and it is why he hears "bottomlessly...one pure thing." We, too, sometimes become aware of the fact that, in the end, despite our manifold encounters with reality, we are facing not a multitude, but a single "Thou" which we therefore call the ONE. We are especially receptive to this insight in moments in which we are listening with the heart to what we have experienced, rather than counting, measuring, assessing or categorizing it. In being touched—rather than in grasping—we can experience two things: that we ourselves are one with the ONE, and that this awareness can heal and unify our inner dividedness.

Think back carefully and in detail to an experience of nature, of a human relationship, of some art that touched you. After-ward, weren't you newly yourself, more at one with yourself? To manage our everyday lives, we need to grasp ideas and gain insight. But we can get bogged down in multiplicity if we don't pay attention to those moments in which we are touched, en-countering the ONE and becoming whole and healed.

67 al-Aḥad
the ONLY ONE

A great deal of damage has been done by the misunderstanding of this name of God. All too often, the ONLY ONE has been played out against "all the others." There could hardly be a more grievous misunderstanding. After all, understood correctly, the ONLY ONE includes all others one could name— there are not actually any others. Any other name could only ever mean the ONLY ONE.

Anyone calling God the ONLY ONE in this sense is committing him- or herself to deepest reverence toward all religions by acknowledging that, despite their various understandings, all religions nevertheless point to the ONLY ONE.

How could it be otherwise? Those who simply parrot names of God they have learned from others are not really naming, but only name-dropping. They are behaving like someone mentioning well-known persons from their circle of acquaintances in order to impress. One essential aspect of naming, however, is a personal relationship. True naming therefore means using traditional names of God to express our own experience of God. However, this deepest, innermost process of connection—such as in peak experiences—requires the insight that the Ultimate Reality is also only one.

These days, one does not need to travel far to learn that people think of and honor the ONLY ONE in many different ways. In any large city, a single glance shows churches and temples of all kinds next to one another. All of humanity's religions are our shared heritage. Can you think of a child close to you whose heart you can open to this heritage, just by offering your own open heart, without saying much? This wealth is worth far more than money in the bank.

68 as-Ṣamad
the INDEPENDENT CAUSE OF ALL

Divine names are actually stammering attempts to address the Ultimate Reality—to call to it, not merely to name it. Naming, after all, seeks to categorize what is named, and in what system could we ever categorize the foundation of all order? We name things, but we address persons. There are then two kinds of naming: like a profile that is impersonal; or face to face with a "Thou."

Lovers are forever playfully giving each other new names. This kind of naming is the kind involved in the divine names. That is why the names of God attain their full resonance only when we put a "Thou" before them. In other words, not "the Merciful," but "Thou Merciful One, who has mercy on me"; not "the Hearing," but "Thou Hearing One, who hears me." Here too: Thou INDEPENDENT CAUSE OF ALL, in whom my own being is laid down infinitely deeply. We are thus addressing the Great Mystery, our fundamental Thou, sensing that this Thou nevertheless infinitely transcends being itself because it neither has nor is being but, instead, is the wellspring of being from which we drink. This experience—and it is crucial—is one that words and names can begin to interpret only after the fact.

The mystical poet Gerhard Tersteegen addresses this INDE-PENDENT CAUSE OF ALL. Can you identify with these lines—from the heart?

> *Air which all inhabits,*
> *At all times surrounds us,*
> *Gives us life and grounds us;*
> *Wonder Thou of wonders,*
> *Deep unending ocean,*
> *Let me sink beneath thy motion.*
> *I in Thee,*
> *Thou in me,*
> *I would vanish fully,*
> *See and find thee truly.*[14]

69 al-Qaadir
the PROVIDENCE, the Power

Unlike other divine names, which can stem from an experience of encountering God, a name such as PROVIDENCE is born of reflection, interpretation, and careful wording. The experiential starting point is brought to mind by the words of a hymn:

> *Praise to the Lord! Who o'er all things*
> *so wond'rously reigneth.*
> *Shelters thee under His wings,*
> *Yea so gently sustaineth;*
> *Hast thou not seen,*
> *How thy desires have been*
> *Granted in what He ordaineth?*[15]

The poetic image of being sheltered beneath a wing may be foreign to us today, but to the question: "Hast thou not seen / how thy desires have been / granted in what He ordaineth?"

we shall probably answer: "Yes, we have seen"—we see and feel so as soon as we awaken and begin to wonder at how our being, despite its fragility and tenuousness, is supported by life. Both are beautifully addressed here: the sense of being supported, led, and sustained on the one hand, and of freedom on the other, in the words, "thy desires." Such a trusting understanding can give meaning to our life story. We may understand PROVIDENCE as a personification as well: God as PROVIDENCE is like a mother, giving us, at the appropriate time, each of those things we need in order to grow and trust—protection and independence.

If we stay close to our experience, which we can because naming and addressing God is praying, not intellectual speculation, then we can call the wellspring of life PROVIDENCE without getting caught in the philosophical snares of free will and predestination. The important question for our peace of heart is: "Hast thou not seen?"

70 al-Muqtadir
the ALL-DETERMINING

Why does this name of God come precisely at this point in our list? It seems that the ALL-DETERMINING was included here to emphasize that divine Providence knows no bounds. In order to understand this name properly, then, it is essential to remember our reflections on the previous name.

Those who confuse providence with predestination will find that, for them, the ALL-DETERMINING becomes the Predetermining—and this freezes and petrifies all spontaneity and living freedom in the icy winds of the cold process of reasoning.

But to those who recognize in the cosmos a practically maternal care for us human beings and therefore call God Providence, the name of the ALL-DETERMINING will mean that the divine diligence over each and every creature, even the lowliest, guarantees its being and its degree of freedom. Who could speak of lowliness then?

The insight that the ALL-DETERMINING has bestowed such great dignity not just on us but, in fact, on everything can help us see the world around us as a world of which we are a part. The fruit of this approach is an awareness of unshakeable security that enables us to grow and fulfill our human lives with supreme joy. Here too, the lines of an old hymn can help us experience this name of God:

> If thou but suffer God to guide thee,
> And hope in Him through all thy ways,
> He'll give thee strength whate'er betide thee.
> And bear thee through the evil days.[16]

Maybe you can look at the mysterious cosmic maternal care that supports and sustains everything, and then call God "loving" as if you had never heard this expression before. But what does "suffer" mean here? Can we prevent this guidance? No, we will be "given strength" and "borne through," even if we worry and mistrust this guidance in the "evil days." But we can entrust these worries to the ALL-DETERMINING, as the hymn continues: "Who trust in God's unchanging love / builds on the rock that nought can move." This includes those who worry unnecessarily!

71 al-Muqaddim
the RIPENER

As I reflect on the individual names of God, I realize more and more clearly that they are evidently due to very different kinds of inspirations. There are first of all those names that we spontaneously give to that unfathomable Mystery which speaks to us through everything that is given. And this mystery lies deeper than all the unsolved mysteries of philosophy and science—in fact, it grows ever more unfathomable to us as our knowledge goes ever deeper. An example of such a name is simply "God," the most general term for that venerable "Thou" we face in every encounter.

But the term "God" for that "Thou," which enables us to say "I," was originally an address, a name—long before it became naming. It is closely related, for example, to the Giver of Life and the Giver of Being. Farther from such immediate experience, it seems, are names such as the Honorer and the Awakener, which already presuppose a great deal of theological terminology. And then there are names that are evidently founded in the up and down of play and interplay between the human "I" and the eternal "Thou,"—the experience of prayer: the All-Hearing One is probably one such name, as is the Withholder. This is the kind of name to which, it seems to me, the RIPENER belongs.

What do you do when it looks like "nothing is moving"? Do you wonder if you've really done everything you can? We shouldn't rush past this question. And do you then also remember that everything needs time to ripen—not just peaches, whose fuzzy cheeks turn red only over time, but decisions, too? Thinking along these lines, and quietly saying the name of the RIPENER to yourself, maybe even several times, full of wonder at the mysterious inner order of all ripening, can become a prayer and transform impatience into true peace of the heart.

72 al-Mu'akhkhir
the DELAYER

This is another name, like the previous one, that must stem from the living encounter with God in prayer. In prayer, I am always standing in the Now—at the intersection of time and eternity. Small as I am, the deeper I am caught up in the past and future, the greater my impatience.

But, just as the impatient "come on!" is resolved as soon as I trust in the Ripener, my anxious "How much longer?" falls silent as soon as I say, smilingly: "O, Thou DELAYER!" It is with an inner smile because I know, deep within me, that delaying and ripening—time itself—are only a pretext for giving us ever-new opportunities. Opportunities for what? Most often, opportunities to learn patience. My Self, the Self that transcends time in the Now, knew this all along.

How long has it been since you last groaned "How much longer?" Often, we don't recognize that kind of sigh as the prayer from the heart that it is. But if we awaken and grow conscious of whom we are actually asking—the DELAYER, who is the only one who can answer it—it can help us reach the difficult point of trusting patience, which doesn't just waste the time we gained by waiting, but actually blossoms in the delay. The twentieth-century Austro-German author, Karl Waggerl, shows us this attitude with a few smiling words through the metaphor of the crocus, which pokes through the snow in late March, when we are already impatient with winter: "God wills it. . . . / And meekly, the crocus / fulfills it."[17]

73 al-Awwal
the FIRST WITHOUT BEGINNING

The FIRST certainly is not meant to be understood as the first link in a chain of other, subsequent components. After all, it is only another name for the Only One. WITHOUT BEGINNING already suggests the Last without End and the Everlasting, bursting the boundaries of all temporal things. We cannot imagine this boundlessness, since all images of our imaginative world are rooted in our dealings with objects in space and time. But, although we cannot picture something without beginning and end, we can nevertheless experience moments to which such words as "beginning" and "end" cannot be applied, because the moments themselves transcend time. Those are also moments that breathe the fresh dew of each first moment, of each fresh start. Each consciously experienced Now is experienced as the first and without beginning.

And do we not experience such a Now whenever we are eye to eye and heart to heart with a dearly beloved person? When

St. Augustine writes of such essential and yet difficult topics, he exclaims: "Give me lovers who shall know what I mean!" So perhaps we should recall our experience as lovers. Can the FIRST WITHOUT BEGINNING be understood perhaps as a name for that mysterious Now in which any deep "I-Thou" encounter takes place, but whose utmost depth is an encounter with God?

Can you remember a moment in your life when love bloomed? Does this memory help you understand our reflections about the FIRST WITHOUT BEGINNING? The German poet Matthias Claudius might have understood them. He wrote:

> *Love knows no bounds, no lock its path defeating;*
> *it anywhere can wend.*
> *It is without beginning. Its wings were ever beating*
> *and beat on without end.*[18]

74 al-Aakḥir
the LAST WITHOUT END

Here too, the preceding name forms a pair with this one. From the perspective of time, we can call our eternal "Thou" the First without Beginning but equally the LAST WITHOUT END. Encountering the First, we recognize ourselves as those ever beginning anew; in the encounter with the Last, we are the unceasingly ending, always ending but never destroyed. Because my true being stands in loving relation to that "Thou," which lives in the eternal Now, I too transcend time. And yet, because this one and only "Thou" gives itself as a gift to all there is, and through this infinite variety gives time as a gift as well, "I," as part of that variety, am also within time. It is for this reason that every moment is to me an intersection of time and eternity. With every passing hour, my "I" passes as well, but my "I-Self" stands eye to eye with my eternal "Thou," breathes the breath of the LAST WITHOUT END, and therefore endures. And that is why the poet, Rilke, says, on the one hand:

I run out, I run out,
as sand running through fingers.[19]

but, on the other hand, says of spring, the metaphor for our loving relationship with the eternal Thou:

Every passing hour grows younger.[20]

Twice now, friends have given me linden trees for my birthday. So far, they are small trees. But I imagine how young couples will sit beneath them, enveloped by their scent, on June evenings when I am long gone. Don't we all want to last? Yes. And our relationship with the LAST WITHOUT END anchors us in the bedrock of eternal being that cannot even be compared to time.

75 aẓ-Ẓaahir
the EVIDENT, the Manifest

In what sense might God be the EVIDENT? To many people nowadays, God is anything other than obvious. But why? Because we imagine a God of hearsay, and our understanding of God is not based on our own experience. So let us ask how God might become evident through our own experience. To do this, we must pay attention to both the inner and outer realms of our experience.

In the outer realm, we experience an unpredictably manifold reality to which we ourselves belong and whose nature becomes to us ever worthier of wonderment, ever more awe-inspiring the more we study it. But this awe and wonderment belong to an inner realm that seems fitted to the outer realm like a cross-section to a surface diagram. The inner realm deals not with the experiencing of objects but with face-to-face encounters with that "Thou" which gives any meaning at all to our saying, "I."

Both the outer and inner experiences, then, confront us with an unfathomable Reality, to which we are oriented through our senses and through our yearning for sense and meaning. It is this Reality which points to the word "God." Starting from personal experience leads us inexorably toward the EVIDENT, who, nevertheless, apparently remains unfathomable.

Have you been lucky enough to discover God through your own experience? Or did well-intentioned others close off your access to a personal encounter with God through their own ideas? If you were lucky, the images others gave you may even have been helpful, especially if you were mature enough not to take them literally. Wherever you are now, you are allowed to— and even have to—start with what is obvious to you. That means that you need to start with your own experience to find the EVIDENT.

76 al-Baatin
the HIDDEN ONE

Why might the HIDDEN ONE be set so closely beside the Evident in this list of names? Perhaps to point to a third reality: belief. Encounter with God, in which all divine names are rooted, becomes truly real only through belief, that is, through the radical trust with which we rely on an Ultimate Reality that confronts us in all that is truly real. But belief as radical trust involves both uncertainty and daring.

If we could not at least sense something of this all-transcending Thou, we could not bear the uncertainty of such reliance. At the same time, if it were not simultaneously hidden, the daring excitement of relying would be lost to us. From our romantic relationships, we human beings are familiar with that joy of life which comes from daring to rely. But we encounter God, the fundamental wellspring of all reality, in every "Thou." Even any human "Thou" becomes more mysterious the more deeply we get to know the person. Awakening to this insight means experiencing the HIDDEN ONE within the Evident and the Evident within the HIDDEN ONE.

Do you use the paths offered by science to encounter the Evident? Nowadays, there are wonderful books and films that teach us grateful wonderment—though only if we see deeply enough through faithful trust to encounter the HIDDEN ONE within the Evident. Any time scientists don't just try to grasp the tangible but dare to be touched by the intangible and unfathomable, science can become an encounter with the whole of reality. This helps us not only to reach goals, but also to find meaning. And that is what human beings need even more urgently.

77 al-Waali
the RULER, the Governor

The RULER fits smoothly into a line of an astoundingly large number of similar names in this list, all of which use the same imagery: God is called the King, the Guardian, the Powerful, the Majestic One, the Most High, the Greatest One, and the Strong One. What might be behind such concerted efforts to point to singular nobility? These names of God most likely spring from the awe and reverence that overwhelm us as human beings when we face the Great Mystery that pervades all things and recognize in it our essential "Thou." In this context, that it is a personal "Thou," and that it governs and effects are both significant. For in the end, instead of a vast influx of data and factoids, our experience of reality finds its focal point in a personal "I-Thou" encounter that orders all things.

Consequently, these names are not in danger of being misused in disparaging comparisons between "one's own" God and those of others, though all religions must constantly guard against the childish temptation of boasting along the lines of: "Ours is greater!" Instead, these names are actually touchingly clumsy attempts to address and call by name that transcendent Reality to which all names point but to which no name can fully do justice.

"Facing the Great Mystery"—does that sound a bit too pompous to fit into your everyday life? It might. But it doesn't depend on your daily life, only on your attitude. Only by learning to engage with the "Thou" that waits to be discovered in every "It" can we awaken our full personhood and find a meaning in life that goes beyond mere goals. And, just like in music, that requires thoughtful pauses. What quiet moments are there in your day?

78 al-Muta'aali
the PURE ONE

It is especially God's most felicitous names that resonate with the awareness of the essential namelessness of the mysterious Reality we are seeking to name. This is the case, too, and indeed especially, with the PURE ONE. The fundamental meaning of "pure" is based on the idea of winnowing out impurities.

But the PURE ONE is not so named because everything apparently impure must be winnowed out from how we imagine God. The reality goes further. Applied to the PURE ONE, "purity" means that what must be winnowed out is imagining God at all, for God is unimaginable. For, as long as what we call by the name of God remains imaginable, it cannot be God. It is at the deepest foundation of all we encounter in the world of imagination or the senses—even in what one or another culture calls impure—that we simultaneously encounter the unimaginable, pure, divine Reality.

Have you ever wondered why we distinguish between pure and impure? When—probably very early—and where—in the context of what culture?—did we learn that distinction? Can we distinguish the PURE ONE in the same way? Why should I be entitled to think that my distinction between pure and impure is based on God? Such questions can help us not only correct our idea of God but also approach people of other traditions. The differences between how we imagine purity become completely unimportant in the face of the PURE ONE—pure of all imagining. Nowadays, the water in some mountain lakes has become so clear again that one can see all the way to the bottom. When we look at the colorful rocks, moss, and fish in the lake, we are also seeing the water. The purer it is, the more invisible it becomes.

79 *al-Barr*
The GOOD ONE

If we assume that divine names come into being by human attempts to say something hesitantly about the utmost Reality to which we have access, "God" (if we even want to use this word), then we may ask: What justifies our calling God "good," and from where then does evil come?

The question is helpful because it is the only way to reach an important insight: When we call God the GOOD ONE, we are refraining from projecting our human ideas of good and evil onto God; rather, we are committing ourselves to constantly learning anew what may truly be called good. We are opening ourselves up to the adventure of always trying and re-trying to read, through God's acts in the world, the meaning of goodness.

In this task, we are once again confronted with two opposing attitudes toward the world—attitudes that must be clearly distinguished: on one level, our knowledge of objects in the

"I-It" relation has primacy; but on a higher level, the insight that our "I-Thou" relationship obtains. One attitude distinguishes, the other sees the oneness of the whole. The "I-It" approach seeks to order, to categorize, to sort into hierarchies; the goal is to distinguish good from evil and choose good. In our "I-Thou" encounters, we simply say Yes to our counterpart. In a very special sense, this Yes "lifts" all contradictions: they remain valid, but are raised to a higher level where they no longer have power.

If we haven't felt this for ourselves, nothing will be able to convince us. But can't you remember moments when life inspired you to an unreserved Yes? In those moments, you know that everything that exists is good. We need the decision and energy of these moments of the "I-Thou" encounter to overcome evil on the "I-It" level in the only way we can: through love. For in the words of the twentieth-century Austro-German poet Will Vesper, "It is by love that everything is good."

80 at-Tawwaab
the ABSOLVER, the Forgiver

Again and again, I find that the names we give God spring from a very specific human experience: we are able to open our hearts so willingly that the foundation of all reality speaks to us in everything and everyone. The most superficial "I-It" relationship can be suddenly breached by the deepest, most touching "I-Thou" encounter. The truer something seems, the more it resonates with me. Reality seems to want to tell me something; perhaps something I do not want to hear—or perhaps something I am longing for.

Freedom is one of the human heart's deepest longings. And in decisive moments, it is this longing to which the ABSOLVER speaks. We want to set out freely, roam freely, be allowed to return home freely—and life accords us all these possibilities. But more: even if we let wishful thinking distract us from our true longing and thus make ourselves unfree, we may still rely on the ABSOLVER.

We can see this in Jesus's parable of the prodigal son, rendered with such incomparable sensitivity by Rembrandt. In faraway lands, the son has sunk to the rank of a lowly swineherd—and then comes to his senses, stands up, and sets out on his journey homeward. Nothing more is needed. All his self-recriminations may fall silent in the arms of the ABSOLVER, who warmly embraces him. And looking closely at the hands of the father in Rembrandt's painting, we find that the artist has given the father a masculine and a feminine hand: in the ABSOLVER, we encounter the maternal love of the Great Mystery.

O THOU, I can hear you when I listen with my heart. You are my freedom. Despite everything that keeps me unfree, give me freedom. Amen.

81 al-Muntaqim
the JUST REQUITER, the Avenger

In whom does the word "requiter" not spark thoughts of revenge? But good can also be requited with good. Those who
were lucky as children were told of a loving God. But many
were also told about an avenging God. Who dreamt up this
terrible force of whom the Hungarian poet, Josef Kis, writes:

*Whose vengeance seven generations runs
through fathers' fathers to the sons of sons?*[21]

Children and all those who do not let their hearts be muddled
know that there can be no such God. Admittedly, if we have
the time to wait long enough, the proverb "Harm set, harm
get" does tend to prove true in the end. To that extent, Goethe
was right to say that "on earth, all is repaid in time"—but
harm takes revenge upon itself! Why then should we accuse
the "heavenly powers"? Goethe's harpist accuses the heavenly
powers with the words, "You let the poor sink into crime." But
he is confusing two worlds: In the "It-world," one stone can
take the next with it, according to the forces of natural laws.
In the "Thou-world," by contrast, freedom and mercy reign.

Now, our world is a single one. The contradiction arises merely through the two ways of looking at it: Seen from the outside, we live in the It-world. The innermost nature of reality, however, is revealed to us in our relationship with the eternal Thou—that is, in the Thou-world. The inner perspective does not invalidate the outer one, but it does give it new meaning. Just as the imprisoned were able to remain free within themselves despite their external confinement, the Thou-world remains free in the midst of the It-world. On earth, all is repaid—or rather, repays itself—in time, but the JUST REQUITER can transform this self-vengeance into mercy.

After all, fault is nothing but wayward longing. The JUST RE-QUITER, however, approaches us and requites even the efforts of our wayward longings by fulfilling them.

O THOU, I long for you, and you approach me full of kindness as the JUST REQUITER of my effortful longing. Amen.

82 al-'Afuww
the Forgiver of Sins, the PARDONER

When we forgive, we offer the offender a great gift: we give up faultfinding—and the accusation is no more to be found. But fault and accusation occur only when "Thou" becomes "It," becomes He or She. We can point an accusatory finger at "that one" or "this one" only if they are "objects of our scorn," that is, if we objectify them. But a "Thou" can never be an object to us, only presence.

We must face up to this Thou, so that the rays of personal encounter can melt those icy accusations into the cleansing waters of forgiveness. Because this transformation proves true in any "I-Thou" relationship, we may dare to call the great "Thou," that is, the final end of any personal relationship, the PARDONER.

But does such a view take faults seriously enough? Yes, and it is in fact the only view that sees what a fault actually consists of—which is to treat a "Thou" as an "It." Accusation does the same, and thus continues the fault; it too requires making a "Thou" into an "It." It is only when we return from fault and accusation to the realm of true "I-Thou" relationship that faults melt away and are pardoned by forgiveness.

O THOU, in myself I stand eye to eye with you. I will try to see you in every face and every face in you, so that I can live for-giveness just as you are forgiveness.

83 ar-Ra'oof
the COMPASSIONATE

Since time immemorial, human hearts have been moved by the question of where suffering originates. "Into life creeps sorrow, as silent as a thief," writes the German poet Joseph von Eichendorff. It "creeps in" because it seems foreign to us; so wholly opposed to what we consider a fulfilled life. But life's fulfillment is always and everywhere part of what human beings call "God." So, how does God stand in relation to suffering?

I can only imagine that life, in all its fullness, simply includes suffering, if only on the level of opposition. On this level, joy and suffering belong to one another, define one another as do light and shadow, mountain and valley. On the level of original oneness, however, all contradictions and opposites are still one, unfolded. There is fullness and nothing amiss. Then, as soon as oneness gives itself to multiplicity, each of the opposites will always be missing its counterpart.

But since the boundless truth we call "God" encompasses both levels, we encounter God—on the level of opposition—in suffering, as well. The COMPASSIONATE is the one who shares in our passion. God is our mother, and does not a mother suffer when she sees her child suffer? She does not suffer "as if" she were feeling that suffering, she feels it, possibly even more painfully than the child itself. The Great Mystery, in its transcendence of time, encompasses—we may even say, embraces—time as well, and therefore, itself suffers if some being somewhere is suffering in some way.

O THOU, my innermost self sometimes senses you as the fullness of life transcending all contradictions in the eternal Now. While I am still in time, let me be connected with you through the oppositions of compassion—fellow suffering and fellow joy. Amen.

84 Maalik ul-Mulk
the Possessor of Royal Sovereignty and Power, the SOVEREIGN

Once again, we have one of the many names apparently resulting from the feeling of facing an overwhelming power. This feeling, after all, is part of any encounter with the Great Mystery, so it should not surprise us that it so often finds expression in the naming of God. As noted in our previous reflections on similar names, we must be particularly careful with this form of divine name, so as not to let it be sullied in our imagination by associations with abuse of power and lead to ideas of God, the SOVEREIGN, as a tyrant in the sky. Such misunderstanding sadly creeps into sermons all too often.

For us human beings, the saying holds true: "Power corrupts." What does that actually mean? In the end, it means that power disempowers all those who come in its sway. However, in the case of God, the SOVEREIGN, it is precisely the opposite: the power of God empowers. Do we not stand taller beneath the starry night sky when, beholding it, we have been overwhelmed by the spirit of the Great Mystery? Do we not walk with more of a spring in our step after the Great Mystery has touched us deeply, for example, in a concert hall listening to Beethoven's Ninth Symphony?

Once we properly understand the kind of power that the name of the SOVEREIGN points to, therefore, we will also understand what we are committing ourselves to in addressing God as powerful. The only just—which is to say, God-oriented—way to use the power we have is to empower all those over whom we exercise power. And we must not be too quick to answer: "Well, but I have no power to exert over anyone!" Any influence is power, and we have influence over a far larger number of people than we might suppose. We therefore honor the SOVEREIGN when we encounter all others in such a way that they feel empowered to do their best—just as we ourselves are empowered in any encounter with the Great Mystery.

Who do you meet throughout your day who looks up to you, listens to you, or trusts you? You have influence over all of them, and it is never too late to realize it. You can turn your power of influence into an honor for the SOVEREIGN by encouraging everyone you encounter to be their best. Yes, even those who try to disempower you. In that way, you are offering them creative resistance.

85 zu-'l-Jalaali wa-'l-Ikraam
the HONORABLE, to whom Majesty and Honor Belong

دُوا لجَلَالٍ وَ الْأَكْرَامِ

Honor is accorded rulers and the powerful all over the world, but they rarely deserve such honor. Let us ask: What would the powerful need to do to earn this honor, to truly deserve it? It might not actually depend so much on their doing as on their being. What might they need to possess in addition to their power? My answer: authority, not mere power. Admittedly, the word "authority" is often misunderstood as the ability to command—but the word comes from the Latin *auctoritas* and eventually the verb *augere*, which loosely means "to increase, enrich, strengthen, grow." This meaning is retained in the English word "augment," meaning "to increase, raise." Authority, then, has the power to increase and strengthen growth.

This can be done only by someone with sufficient insight to counsel others in doubt. A good example might be the old woman in the village whom one asks about home remedies, or a doctor who is seen as "an authority" and therefore consulted for a second opinion. It is in this sense, augmented to infinity, that we can call the "King of Glory" the HONORABLE, worthy of highest honor and authority.

It is from the authority of the Great Mystery that all insight for correct action flows down to us. Our capacity for listening, for insight, and for translating insight into action is what gives us dignity. When we succeed, it seems effortless. And it is, to the extent that in that moment we can let go of our usual efforts to make the right decision and put it into practice. But this letting go demands more of us than any effort. As we succeed in it, however, we are literally honoring the HONORABLE in our deeds.

Before you make your next small or large decision, take a moment to listen closely to the things life is giving you in that instant. Aren't they mysterious enough to give you trust that they are encounters with the Great Mystery here and now, and that the authority of the HONORABLE wants to guide you? Open yourself up to that guidance without being distracted by hopes, wishes, or fears. Trust in that guidance, and you will not be disappointed.

86 al-Muqsiṭ
the EQUITABLE JUDGE

In our reflections on the name of God the Judge, we already pointed out that we must, under no circumstances, project onto God, the image of a judge from an earthly courtroom— not even the idea of a fair judge. A fair judge may do their best, but they too are caught up in a justice system where the idea of criminal justice does not right wrongs, but enacts revenge. God, as the EQUITABLE JUDGE, does not avenge, but makes right. This point is so important that, in addition to the Judge and the Just, the EQUITABLE JUDGE is added to the list of 99 names as the one righting wrongs.

"Vengeance is mine," says the EQUITABLE JUDGE (Romans 12:19). We may leave it to God, for in the hands of the EQUI-TABLE JUDGE vengeance becomes something else, something life-affirming, healing, and reconciliatory.

In the ballad "Feet to the Fire" by the German poet Conrad Ferdinand Meyer a king's courier seeks refuge from a storm, asking at the nearest castle he can find whether he may stay the night. He is hospitably received and realizes too late that he has inadvertently entered into the house of the nobleman whose wife he tortured to death some years ago in a search for traitors. He locks the door to his bedchamber, but nevertheless passes a sleepless night in fear. In the morning, the nobleman enters through a secret door. It would have been easy for him to avenge the murder of his wife. Instead, he rides with the courier part of the way. As he departs, the courier unabashedly praises the nobleman's wise restraint: after all, as a messenger from the King of France, the courier is "the greatest King's own." "Indeed," replies the nobleman, "the greatest King's own"—meaning, however, the EQUITABLE JUDGE:

> Indeed! The greatest king's own! Today,
> His service pressed me hard . . . Fiendishly thou
> murdered my wife—and live! . . .
> Mine is vengeance, saith the Lord.[22]

What it cost the nobleman to place his vengeance in the hands of the Lord is shown by his hair, which has turned from brown to gray in the night passed grappling with the decision.

Maybe you can find a translation of this entire poem and read it today. Or just consider what might have moved the nobleman to choose as he did. Remember that those who forgive are fulfilling the healing "vengeance" of the EQUITABLE JUDGE, who rights wrong.

87 al-Jaami'
the GATHERER, the Uniter

As a young monk, I had one of those dreams that one does not forget as long as one lives: world and time had ended. I was a child, running to find my grandmother and telling her joyfully: "They have all come together!" Again and again, I called out to her, thrilled: "They have all come together!"

Little wonder, then, that the name of the GATHERER recalls this dream to me with wonderment, especially given the additional meaning of the Arabic: "who shall gather all people on the Last Day." Is not deep within us all a longing that, at least at the end but one hopes before, our human family will overcome all enmities and live together in harmony? "Hail to the Spirit that may join us," calls out Rilke, but:

> *Before there was to die, there was to slay.*
> *A gash tore through your ripened orbs,*
> *up went a cry.*
> *Those voices torn away*
> *only just assembling*
> *to say you,*

relay you,
bridge across all chasms.
And what they stammer, trembling,
have since been spasms
of your ancient name.[23]

Aghast, the poet bewails such splintering. The GATHERER, however, is forgiving, healing, and unifying. On that we may rely—and prove our trust by ourselves doing what we can to further peace and understanding in our families, in our communities, and among all the people of the world.

Lord, make me an instrument of your peace,
where there is hate, let me sow love;
where there is injury, pardon;
where there is discord, unity.

Whenever we pray these words of the Prayer of St. Francis, we are praying in the spirit of the GATHERER.

88 al-Ghaniyy
the WEALTHY ONE,
the Self-Sufficient

A child owes everything to its mother: its life, its love, even the pocket money with which it buys its mother a small gift. And yet the gift brings the mother great joy, which she could not have made for herself. In the same way, we return everything we have been given to God, the WEALTHY ONE, the one who needs no one—and give it back transformed. Here of all places, paradoxically, it is true that God needs humankind.

Rilke speaks of the "superfluity of all things" flowing into God "when things and thoughts run over"—in other words, when "our heart is overflowing," as one says, at a moving sight, and then what we have seen, transformed by our unique experience, streams back into the Great Mystery from whose wealth it was given to us. Rilke shows us what he means using the example of art, praying:

And painters paint for that one reason:
That nature, which you made to fade in season,
should be unfading given back to you.[24]

But it is not just artists who make the fleeting eternal, the fading unfading. To us all, that is the highest purpose in life. We as human beings belong to the fading and fleeting, but reach into the mystery, into the eternal and unfading. Everything that our senses grasp flows through us, and through us returns into the ungraspable mystery. It is for this reason that Rilke calls us "the bees of the universe": through everything we do and experience, we gather the nectar of the visible into the great golden honeycomb of the Invisible. This image shows the stream of blessing as flowing back—and the WEALTHY ONE appears so abundantly rich only because the given riches are unceasingly flowing back enriched:

> *So flows the superfluity of things to you.*
> *And like the highest fountain basin stands*
> *forever overflowing, as with strands*
> *of loosened hair dropping down beneath,*
> *so falls the fullness from you to your heath*
> *when things and thoughts run over.*[25]

You are unique. No one has ever seen a tree exactly the way you do. Everything you were born with and all your life experiences are part of how you look at things. Today, maybe you can silently look at a tree for a while and enjoy that you enrich the universe, and that you are returning the tree to the WEALTHY ONE, richer for your gaze.

89 al-Mughni
the GIVER OF RICHES

All the blessings of the world, all that we have and are, every-thing is unceasingly flowing to us from the inexhaustible wellspring of being, that is, from the Wealthy One. We learned this in reflecting on the previous name. And now we come upon a paradox: the GIVER OF RICHES is eternally giving Him-self to others as a gift, and Rilke is right to pray:

> You are the poor, the penniless of those...
> All yours is nothings, wind so barely known;
> Your glory hardly shields your nudity,
> Even an orphan's unregarded gown
> is lovelier and more like property.[26]

Is that merely a poetic play on the idea that all opposites co-incide in God? No, it is the expression of a deep insight: all things in which the GIVER OF RICHES gives Himself away are richness, even poverty itself. And so even poverty can become wealth to us if we understand it as a gift from God.

Recognizing the GIVER OF RICHES in the "golden over-abundance of the world" is easy, even obvious. But sensing his presence in all that which is poor requires growth of the heart. We should not let ourselves be tempted to romanticize poverty with sweet sentiment—on the contrary, we must do everything we can to reduce it and change the social system that produces poverty. But we will encounter the poor very differently if we recognize in them the GIVER OF RICHES, to whom Rilke prays:

> You are the utmost penniless of those,
> The beggar, his face hidden from gaze
> and shrouded, poverty's great rose...[27]

Today, look into the eyes of a beggar—that alone is a gift—and consciously encounter there the GIVER OF RICHES, who gives Himself away.

90 al-Maani'
the WITHHOLDER,
the Refuser

A teacher asks a schoolgirl: "What do you need your reason for?" She answers without hesitation: "To keep secrets." Clearly, to her, "reason" means more than common sense. She uses it to mean her entire inner life. That is why her answer is so apposite: it awakens our awareness of our inner life as something that refuses any access from the outside—that holds something back. This mysterious withholding, which protects and preserves our innermost dignity, is part even of our most intimate personal relationships—indeed, belongs especially to them, and it is from this experience that the WITHHOLDER as the name for our divine Thou can be explained.

> *Into thy name's most ancient night*
> *did delve a thousand theologians...*[28]

But no name can illuminate the darkness of the unfathomable beyond the boundaries of such withholding. Nikolaus Lenau, an Austrian Romantic poet, uses the same image of night to invoke the unfathomable nature of the WITHHOLDER, praying:

Dwell upon me, thou dark eye,
exercise thy utter might,
somber, gentle, musing, dreamy,
sweet unfathomable night![29]

We may imagine the night of the WITHHOLDER as sweet, not frightening—for in the end, it is that unfathomability which is part of learning to trust in any loving relationship. And this experience of trust in unfathomability makes it easier for us to deal with those moments when the WITHHOLDER answers our wishes with a No. For we must not forget that our daily life is nothing other than a constant array of opportunities for encountering the nameless Mystery behind all divine names. "No fate, no rejection, no hardship is simply hopeless," writes Rilke. "Somewhere, the harshest briar can yield leaves, a blossom, a fruit. And somewhere in God's outermost providence, there will already be an insect, too, that bears riches away from this flower..." Trusting in the WITHHOLDER, we may ourselves be those bees that suck sweetness even from the blossoms of withholding and refusal.

What does life seem to be refusing you? If you lift your eyes to the WITHHOLDER, can you turn it into the honey of trust?

91 aḍ-Ḍharr
the HARMER

How can we call God the HARMER? Only in the deepest trust that even all those things that harm us are a gift of love. This radical trust in life is about an attitude of complete oneness—with oneself and with the eternal Mystery—an attitude, in the words of T. S. Eliot, "costing not less than everything."[30]

Many people say: "I believed in God until such and such happened to me. Since then I haven't been able to believe in God." Here, a collapse of faith has been caused by something that actually could have been an impulse for the radical realization of believing trust. We cannot know for certain in advance whether, under a painful blow, our faith will shatter or begin in earnest. But we can be prepared! Just as we can learn to trust through our reflections on the inscrutability of the Withholder, we can learn to understand that the HARMER, too, can be a name for God. This is easier when we look not at ourselves but at the whole, for benefit and detriment can apply only to aspects. But when we look at the whole, both detriment and benefit are gains—a gain in being.

But, as already noted, making the great choice to open our heart to the fullness of being costs us "not less than everything." Here too, we find that, by looking at the whole, we will praise the whole.

> Don't suppose falsely that there could be any
>   privation
> for that decreed resolution, which was that you be!
> Silken thread, you became part of the woven creation.
> With whichever image you may have been linked at
>   the heart,
> (and be it a second in life full of agony),
> feel: what is meant is the whole of the tapestry's art.[31]

Where does the HARMER challenge you most? Take it as an impulse to choose radical trust. It is the choice between an embittered and a fulfilled life.

92 an-Naafi'
the BENEFACTOR

Benefit and detriment are relative terms, dependent on circumstances. For snow hares, their beautiful white coat would
be a detriment in a green summer meadow. What is the purpose of these reflections? First, the BENEFACTOR is a divine
name that is relevant only within a relative area of our experience. In those moments in which we can sense the Ultimate
Reality, we become conscious of the fact that the BENEFACTOR
does not play favorites. This opens up another insight: if the
All-Encompassing, the Bestower, and the Giver—as he is described by other names in our list—bestows any benefits on
us in any way, then they are always also a gift of the opportunity to help others who have not benefited in the same way,
sharing as an equalizing justice. Indeed, we are already
drawn to this gift by the empathy with which we and other
higher animals are born.

Searching the internet for the terms "chocolate for the first time," we can find short films that let us see cocoa bean farmers on the Ivory Coast tasting their first bite of the product that they work so hard for every day. At first, we laugh at the surprised joy on the black faces and at a worker's suggestion that perhaps chocolate might be the reason why white people live so long. But then the workers have shared out between them and eaten what may be the only bar of chocolate they will see in their lives, and one of them wants to take home at least the wrapper, to show his children. The laughter catches in our throat—even more so when one thinks of the extent to which harvesting cocoa beans relies on child labor.

Today, maybe you will have an opportunity to tell that story— of the children on the Ivory Coast and how hard they have to work in the cocoa plantations—to a child that has never thought about where chocolate comes from. Knowing about these problems is the first step to improving them.

93 an-Nur
the LIGHT

Is my consciousness the only lit window in the night of an impersonal universe? Or does my conscious being, like a mirror, reflect the light shining throughout the entire universe? However we may answer this question, almost no one will object to the use of light as a metaphor for consciousness. We even describe those with particularly keen consciousness as "enlightened." And because the light of human self-consciousness is in reference to the divine Thou, it seems obvious to use the same metaphor of light for God as well. This is why many spiritual traditions speak of our encounters with the Ultimate Reality in terms of illumination and enlightenment, and of the Great Mystery as the LIGHT.

But at the same time, darkness can also appear as a fitting image for the Great Mystery—in describing its unfathomable nature. Finding it hard to choose between these two images merely points, once more, to God as the place where all opposites coincide in oneness.

The prologue to the Gospel of John explores even more deeply this reconciliation of contradictory opposites by stating that "the light shines in the darkness" (John 1:5). This would be hardly worth mentioning if taken to mean merely that light shines into darkness as a kind of searchlight. Instead, what is being said is something unheard of: that the LIGHT of God is not light being shined *into* darkness, but a shining light *within* darkness itself.

From this mystical insight we may therefore take deep comfort. All that occurs to us in our daily lives is seeking to become encounter with God, and so we may say even to the darkest moment: "Be my LIGHT!"

Will you dare try this in one of your darkest experiences? It won't make the darkness light. Darkness will remain dark, but radical trust walks bravely into darkness and finds the LIGHT in the middle of it.

94 al-Haadi
the GUIDE

In the Christian tradition, too, we pray for God as a guide—to "Lead, Kindly Light," as an old hymn expresses it. From what common experience have people of wholly different eras and cultures drawn the idea that God is the GUIDE? Before any large or small decision, any person who practices pausing for a moment and listening to what is given in that moment will, again and again, encounter the GUIDE. This is true for all decisions that must be made: from daily plans to the hardest choices—through the given circumstances alone, life is already showing us the way. Hopes and fears, wishes, objections, expectations may whirl wildly about amid possibilities and obstacles. But if we watch mindfully and with trust, then the maelstrom subsides and a still, clear current begins to reveal itself.

What is offering this guidance is the Great Mystery, for it is the source from which life, with all its overwhelming array of options, streams toward us. Who would be capable of logically tallying up all the arguments and counterarguments for their choice? But deep in our innermost center of being, we can become aware of what Ignatius of Antioch describes so fittingly: "There is within me a water that liveth and speaketh, saying to me inwardly, Come to the Father" (Ign. Romans 7:2).[32] Instead of water, Rilke uses the image of wind to describe the same experience:

> Ah, not to be cut off,
> not separated by such paltry walls
> from the measure of the stars.
> Innermost, what is it,
> If not heightened heaven
> streaked through with birds and deeply
> by winds of return home.[33]

Understanding this return home as a flight from the world would be a grave mistake. Our home is not elsewhere: the GUIDE is close to us when we are on the path amid our search for direction, leading us through the constellation of all inner and outer motivations. Being at home means being inwardly at one with oneself and thus also with the GUIDE.

"Homeward is the direction of all paths."[34] *Are you ready to be guided by practicing silent listening?*

95 al-Badee'
the CREATOR OF THE NEW

Who does not welcome a fresh start?

One feels the shine of a new page
on which all may yet become.[35]

The more mindful we become, the more consciously we can perceive every moment as a fresh start. The CREATOR OF THE NEW is allowing us a role in the process through which, in every moment, something new is becoming reality from the inexhaustible supply of potentiality. "Nothing was fulfilled before I glimpsed it"[36]—because my looking, here and now, is a wholly unique event. No one has ever seen with eyes that are identical to mine. If my fingerprint is already unique, how much more my nervous system! All the impressions that a pear, for example, has ever made on me have influenced how I see, smell, and savor this pear today. The next time I look, today's experience will inform that look as well— the pear will once again be never-before-seen in a wholly new way.

Looking is always also an act of selection. From the welter of impressions, we subconsciously choose what speaks to us, and through our feeling and thinking we transform it into something that has never been before. What we gain from the welter is our personal contribution to the whole of reality, and that contribution depends on whether we coldly acknowledge the world or welcome it with blessings and thus pass it on as a gift into the great stream of blessing, the universe's blood-stream. Such is the magnitude of the responsibility with which the CREATOR OF THE NEW entrusts us. Rilke, too, sings of this great stream:

> *What our spirits from the torrent gain*
> *will sometime be to all of life's improvement.*
> *And if by some chance only thoughts remain,*
> *they seep into that stream of lifeblood's movement*
> *flowing amain...*
>
> *And if but feelings: who can know their reach*
> *and what they may yet yield in that pure space*
> *in which some added weight or lightness each*
> *can alter worlds or move stars from their place.*[37]

Today, make your senses wide and welcoming, conscious of how that connects you with the CREATOR OF THE NEW. Open yourself to this feeling of spring, and enjoy it. It keeps you young.

96 al-Baaqi
the EVERLASTING

Does new always mean better? Advertising would have us believe so. And if we wait long enough, then the present—romantically tinged by memory—becomes the good old days. But what we really long for in the deepest depths of our hearts is not dependent on old or new. When our longing speaks of old or new, it is referring to something that transcends both: the everlasting. As Nietzsche says: "Delight wants for all things eternity...deepest, deepest eternity."[38]

> *Tremulous, we long to find a hold;*
> *Too young, we sometimes long for what is old,*
> *too old, we long for things that never were.*[39]

This hold that we—caught up in the inexorable strides of history—long for so desperately can be found only in the EVERLASTING.

> *Castaways we—*
> *But take time's measured tread*
> *As inconsequent shred*
> *Of eternity.*[40]

It is to the EVERLASTING that Rilke prays:

> *I read it in your word,*
> *In all the gestures' history*
> *with which your hands, cupped guidingly*
> *around becoming, wisdom warm endowed.*
> *You spoke death soft and life aloud*
> *And always and again repeated: Be.*[41]

I can sense this being when I entrust myself to the EVERLASTING in whose hands my being finds repose, whether I live or die. This entrusting of oneself is called prayer. When we look at a chessboard, we can see either black squares on a white background or white squares on a black background—praying means looking at the double realm of reality in such a way that the eyes of the heart, which are used to seeing only the ephemeral, attend to the EVERLASTING and find there the relief of peace.

We should not expect to see the EVERLASTING in prayer. What is visible is only the ephemeral. But we can let the EVERLASTING act upon us. This is why Gerhard Tersteegen prays:

> *Thou who all pervadest;*
> *Let thy light so comely*
> *play upon my visage warmly.*
> *As the tender blossoms*
> *willingly unfolding,*
> *to the sun their faces holding:*
> *Thus let me*
> *joyously*
> *silent, Thy beams capture,*
> *that Thou me enrapture.*[42]

97 al-Waarit
the HEIR,
for Nothing Else but Him is Lasting

Is it not astounding that, across completely different cultures and far-flung periods of history, the human spirit has addressed the Great Mystery in names that are so similar to one another? This is true even of such an apparently outlandish name as the HEIR. Rilke, writing in nineteenth-century Germany almost certainly without ever having heard the name al-Waarit, prays:

You are the heir.
The son is the heir,
Father no longer there.
Sons stand and bloom.
You are the heir.[43]

To illustrate what he means, he then offers a long list of ephemeral things and experiences which, by his memory, have entered into the realm of the unfading and eternal. "So flows the superfluity of things to you," he says to God, and so its eternal wellspring also becomes its everlasting HEIR: "All things fulfilled will devolve." The word, "devolve," is simultaneously a term from the legal field of inheritance law.

However the world may evolve
like clouds unfold,
all things fulfilled will devolve
back home to the age-old.[44]

Our remembering plays a decisive part in this process. Mere recall is limited to the external, but memory and remembrance involve internalization. In the double realm in which we human beings live, the outer and inner world, fading and unfading, are distinguishable but nevertheless one—just like "I" and "Self." Recall can only represent what the eyes have taken in, but memory sees with the heart. And so to memory, the sensuous becomes a sign with a sense, that is to say, meaning. The heart reads this meaning in the ephemeral and destructible and preserves it as indestructible. From God as the wellspring of meaning and sense, sense flows into all that can be grasped with the senses. We may draw on it and let the meaning, the sense, flow back to God the HEIR.

My heart, oh say,
what memories you weave
in the twilight of gold-green leaves?
– Ancient unknowable days![45]

These words are by the German poet Eduard Mörike. What memories do you weave? When you internalize them to memory, it is as if you are communicating them to the great Thou. You can now never lose them, because you are sharing them with their eternal HEIR.

98 ar-Rasheed
the GIVER OF GUIDANCE

If God is the Guide, then God's guidance is given to us: as a gift, and as a responsibility. We may rely on it. This guidance is not, as on the stage of classical theater, set up in contrast to seduction: the GIVER OF GUIDANCE and the Seducer are not struggling to gain a human soul. Instead, we ourselves are given to struggle, and that struggle, in the end, is our inner struggle to trust. As long as we can trustingly follow the guidance we are given, every path leads home, and every step is a homecoming. But as soon as fear deafens us to guidance, every path misleads us.

Letting oneself be led requires trust, but fear makes us recalcitrant. Fear, on the one hand, twists us inside. Like the twisted Bøyg tells Ibsen's Peer Gynt, "Round about!" fear offers us the same advice whenever something frightens us. Twisted thinking does not admit its own fear and leads to self-deception; twisted feeling shuts out all that frightens and becomes sentimentality. In the end, the path of fear leads to a life lived in lies.

Trust, on the other hand, straightens our inner stance, makes us sober in thinking and honest in feeling; frank and forthright. In all that we do, we are "gently sustained" by the GIVER OF GUIDANCE.

How can we learn to trust? With practice! When anxieties come, do not fear, but walk trustingly into their narrows. The word "anxiety" is etymologically related to painful tightness and narrowness. Fear resists that anxiety and gets stuck in the narrowness. Instead, if we trust, the narrowness of anxiety becomes like a birth canal for a fresh start. Try that today on an anxiety that is easy to conquer. Step by step, you can practice approaching bigger and bigger anxieties.

99 aṣ-Ṣaboor
the PATIENT ONE

Naming God always begins at one or another of comparatively few starting points. This is easy to see when we reflect on this list of 99 names of God: on the one hand, there are those names the heart calls out when it senses the Great Mystery, and on the other hand, those that clearly originate in theological speculation. But in the end, any naming of God, whether from the heart or from the head, is based on an encounter with God. And to us human beings, those are inescapably given. We do not know whether this is the case with animals, but the Bedouin claim that only the camel knows the 100th name of Allah most likely comes from someone who was deeply impressed by these animals' meditative bearing, motionlessly dreaming out at the vastness of the desert through long-lashed, gentle eyes. But perhaps there was also a suspicion that animals, in ways we cannot even imagine, sense something of the Great Mystery.

For human beings, it is from this sensing that the urge to name springs. The theologically cogitated names probably include ones such as the Independent Cause of All. But, "it is the heart that senses God, not reason." Reason lags behind. That is why far more of the names point to qualities that the heart admires in human beings and ascribes to the "wonder of wonders": royal transcendence, paternal steadfastness, but above all, maternal, all-embracing love and patience.

The PATIENT ONE must look on all these names with a patient, half-amused, half-exasperated smile, just as I remember my mother doing when she would rest at the side of the wheat field and allow us children to "decorate" her by sticking flowers and pretty blades of grass in her hair. In the same way, with childlike love and childish ineptitude, we nevertheless name the one who transcends all names. And the maternally PATIENT ONE is pleased to go along with this, and even, we trust, takes a little pleasure in it.

HE lets Himself be glimpsed in the letters

In Arabic, a zero is signified by a dot. This dot is the beginning of all things—and of all writing, as well. Is it really just a dot? Could it not also be a burn, a seed, a drop, a crumb, a birthmark, a diamond, a bud, a tear, or nothingness? *He formed Non-Being into Being. Who but He could make Being from Nothing?* (Sa'di, Iran, 13th century). Certainly, through the movement of a single point, of this Nothing, all being is created. If the dot moves downward, connecting heaven and earth, it forms the first letter of the Arabic alphabet: *Alif.*

Alif, the first letter of the word *Allah*. The mystic Hafiz (Iran, 14th century) is fascinated by the mystery of this letter: *On the tablet of my heart is written nothing but an Alif, the shape of a friend. What shall I do, my master has taught me no other letter.*

Alif, the shape of a friend, also suggests a swaying cypress, a gaunt fakir, an unadorned, ascetic dervish, or an arrow.

If the dot is lengthened horizontally from right to left, it makes the second letter of the alphabet: *Ba*. Is this letter not a supplication of the servant of God before the *Alif* at the beginning of the word *Allah*? Combining the vertical *Alif* with the horizontal *Ba* gives the ancient symbol of the cross. God lets himself be glimpsed in the letters. Sometimes, the diacritical mark below the letter *Ba* is called the most beautiful name of God. Calligraphy becomes a divine art and the expression of divine beauty.

> *"God is beautiful and loves beauty."* (Hadith [saying of the Prophet], related by Saheeh Muslim)

It would take too long to introduce all letters with respect to their outer form. The calligrapher uses these outer characteristics, combines and varies the letters in such a way that the text becomes like an image—without pushing that image too far to the fore. Calligraphy remains as an image without image, a silent music: truly a bridge between hand and heart. It is in fact "the language of the hand and the joy of the heart" (Ali ibn Abi Talib, 7th century). This connection should be imbued by the flow of the spirit, which is the source of the spirit.

This mutual relationship between hand, heart, and head is what earns calligraphy its high rank within the Islamic arts. It was born of the necessity of artfully communicating both sacred and profane knowledge and wisdom. Its theoretical basis lies in Vedic mathematics, philosophy, and cosmology. Calligraphy is a strict science, seen as "half of the wisdom" itself. And yet, the mystery of the letters remains: "Are not people themselves mysterious cyphers, waiting in heaven for their appearance in this world, as if to become part of the vast book of the universe?" asks the mystic Ibn Arabi (Spain, 12th century).

So, four years ago, when my friend Brother David asked me to develop calligraphies for the 99 names of God, I joyously and unhesitatingly said Yes. Immediately two memories—one of childhood, the other from my days as a student—rose up within me. As a boy, I was interested in discovering the highest, most beautiful names of God. Perhaps then, I thought, I would be able to pierce life's mysteries, even transmute the base metal of my being into gold: an alchemy of happiness. Patiently, my father tried to explain that there were countless ways of referring to God, in one treatise even as many as 999. The Qur'an alone contains 84. Many mystics are satisfied with the simple address "*Hu*," meaning "He." In their multiplicity, His names form unity.

The second memory comes from my time as a student, when I was engaging with the works of the mystic Najmad-din Alkubra (Iran, 13th century). A score of students surrounded the great master in order to be told the most beautiful name of God. The master had his grandchild on his lap and was playing with it. As the students impatiently all but harangued him to give them the longed-for answer, the master lifted up the child and said: "The greatest is You, the most beautiful is You." In the beauty of a butterfly, the smile of a child, the silence of the mountains: all the cosmos sings through Him. Everything is a sign of God. As the mystic Bayazid Bistami (Iran, 10th century) puts it aptly: "For thirty years, I was always speaking God's name. When I fell silent, I understood that the wall separating me from Him was naming."

For this book, I have created calligraphies of the 99 names of God and the term "Allah" using three script varieties—namely, *Thuluth*, *Nastaliq*, and *Shekasteh*, that is, curved, hanging, and broken styles. May the beauty and oneness of God be glimpsed in them. I would like to close with a verse of the Mughal mystic, poet, and calligrapher Darah Shukoh (India, 17th century): "In the name of Him who has no name, such as you call Him, such shall He appear."

—Shams Anwari-Alhosseyni

Notes

1. Matthias Claudius, "Täglich zu singen" [To sing daily], *Der Wandsbecker Bote* [The Wandsbeck Messenger], 121, trans. by Peter Dahm Robertson.

2. Joseph von Eichendorff, "Der Pilger" [The Pilgrim], no. 3, trans. by Peter Dahm Robertson.

3. Benjamin Schmolck, "Amen! Amen!" 1723, trans. by Peter Dahm Robertson.

4. Angelus Silesius (Johann Scheffler), "Die Gottheit ist ein Nichts" [The godhead is a nought], *Der Cherubinische Wandersmann* [The Cherubinic Wayfarer], 111, trans. by Peter Dahm Robertson.

5. Rainer Maria Rilke, "Herbst" [Fall], September 11, 1902, trans. by Peter Dahm Robertson.

6. Claudius, "Täglich zu singen" [To sing daily], trans. by Peter Dahm Robertson.

7. Friedrich Nietsche, "Dem unbekannten Gott" [To the unknown God], September 1864, trans. by Peter Dahm Robertson.

8. Rainer Maria Rilke, *Duineser Elegien* [Duino Elegies], "First Elegy," January 1912, trans. by Peter Dahm Robertson.

9. Rainer Maria Rilke, "Du bist so groß," [You are so great], August 26, 1899, trans. by Peter Dahm Robertson.

10. Rainer Maria Rilke, *Das Stundenbuch*, "Das Buch vom

mönchischen Leben" [The Book of Hours: The Book of Monkish Living], 1899, trans. by Peter Dahm Robertson.

11. Rainer Maria Rilke, *Die Sonette an Orpheus* [The Sonnets to Orpheus], Part 2: 23, 1922, trans. by Peter Dahm Robertson.

12. Rilke, *Die Sonette an Orpheus*, Part 1: 12, 1922, trans. by Peter Dahm Robertson.

13. Rilke, *Die Sonette an Orpheus*, Part 2: 15, 1922, trans. by Peter Dahm Robertson.

14. Gerhard Tersteegen, "Gott ist gegenwärtig" [God is present], 1729, trans. by Peter Dahm Robertson.

15. Joachim Neander, "Lobe den Herren" [Praise to the Lord], 1665, trans. by Catherine Winkworth, in *The Chorale Book for England*, ed. William Sterndale Bennet and Otto Goldschmidt (London: Longman, Green, Longman Roberts, and Green, 1863). Accessed through: https://archive.org/details/choralebookfore00winkgoog/page/n42/mode/2up, last accessed August 1, 2020.

16. Georg Neumark, "Wer nur den lieben Gott lässt walten" [If thou but suffer God to guide thee], 1641, trans. by Catherine Winkworth, in *The Chorale Book for England*, ed. William Sterndale Bennet and Otto Goldschmidt (London: Longman, Green, Longman Roberts, and Green, 1863). Accessed through: https://archive.org/details/choralebookfore00winkgoog/page/n264/mode/2up, last accessed August 1, 2020.

17. Karl Heinrich Waggerl, *Heiteres Herbarium* [Jolly Herbarium], trans. by Peter Dahm Robertson.

18. Matthias Claudius, "Die Liebe hemmet nichts" [Love knows no bounds], 1798, trans. by Peter Dahm Robertson.

19. Rilke, "Das Buch vom mönchischen Leben," trans. by Peter Dahm Robertson.

20. Rilke, *Die Sonette an Orpheus*, Part 2, 25, trans. by Peter Dahm Robertson.

21. Josef Kis, as translated by Hedwig Lachmann, "Jehovah, Erste Fassung" [Jehova, First Version], in *Gesammelte Gedichte: Eigenes und Nachdichtungen* [Collected Poems: Own and Translations] (Potsdam: Gustav Kiepenheuer Verlag, 1919). Accessed through: https://archive.org/details/gesammeltegedich00lachuoft/page/360/mode/2up, last accessed August 3, 2020. Trans. from the German by Peter Dahm Robertson.

22. Conrad Ferdinand Meyer, "Die Füße im Feuer" [Feet to the Fire], 1882, trans. by Peter Dahm Robertson.

23. Rilke, "Das Buch vom mönchischen Leben," trans. by Peter Dahm Robertson.

24. Rainer Maria Rilke, *Das Stundenbuch*, "Das Buch der Pilgerschaft" [The Book of Hours: The Book of Pilgrimage], 1901, trans. by Peter Dahm Robertson.

25. Rilke, "Das Buch der Pilgerschaft" [The Book of Pilgrimage], trans. by Peter Dahm Robertson.

26. Rainer Maria Rilke, *Das Stundenbuch*, "Das Buch von der Armut und vom Tode" [The Book of Hours: The Book of Poverty and of Death], 1903, trans. by Peter Dahm Robertson.

27. Rilke, "Das Buch von der Armut und vom Tode" [The Book of Poverty and of Death], trans. by Peter Dahm Robertson.

28. Rilke, "Das Buch vom mönchischen Leben," trans. by Peter Dahm Robertson.

29. Nikolaus Lenau, "Weil' auf mir, du dunkles Auge" [Dwell upon me, thou dark eye], trans. by Peter Dahm Robertson.

30. T. S. Eliot, "Little Gidding," from *Four Quartets*, 1940.

31. Rilke, *Die Sonette an Orpheus*, Part 2, 21, trans. by Peter Dahm Robertson.

32. Taken from *The Early Church Fathers and Other Works*, Wm. B. Eerdmans Pub. Co., 1867, as reproduced at https://www.catholicculture.org/culture/library/view.cfm?recnum=3836, accessed July 22, 2020.

33. Rainer Maria Rilke, Literary Estate: *Completed Poems*, 1925, trans. by Peter Dahm Robertson.

34. Rilke, Literary Estate: *Completed Poems*, 1925, trans. by Peter Dahm Robertson.

35. Rilke, "Das Buch vom mönchischen Leben," trans. by Peter Dahm Robertson.

36. Rainer Maria Rilke, "Da neigt sich die Stunde" [The hour inclines], September 20, 1899, trans. by Peter Dahm Robertson.

37. Rilke, Literary Estate: *Dedications: "Für Fräulein Marga Wertheimer"* [For Miss Marga Wertheimer], 1924, trans. by Peter Dahm Robertson.

38. Nietzsche, *Also Sprach Zarathustra* [Thus Spoke Zarathustra], vol. 4, "Das Nachtwandler-Lied" [The Song of the Night-Wanderer], Part 11, trans. by Peter Dahm Robertson.

39. Rilke, *Die Sonette an Orpheus*, Part 2: 23, trans. by Peter Dahm Robertson.

40. Rilke, *Die Sonette an Orpheus*, Part 1: 22, trans. by Peter Dahm Robertson.

41. Rilke, "Das Buch vom mönchischen Leben," trans. by Peter Dahm Robertson.

42. Tersteegen, "Gott ist gegenwärtig" [God is present], trans. by Peter Dahm Robertson.

43. Rilke, "Das Buch der Pilgerschaft," trans. by Peter Dahm Robertson.

44. Rilke, *Die Sonette an Orpheus*, Part 1: 19, trans. by Peter Dahm Robertson.

45. Eduard Mörike, *Gedichte* [Poems], 1838, trans. by Peter Dahm Robertson.

Biographies

David Steindl-Rast

David Steindl-Rast was born 1926 in Vienna and studied at the Akademie der Bildenden Künste and the University of Vienna. After a doctorate in psychology and anthropology, he immigrated to the United States, where, since 1953, he has been a member of the Mount Saviour Benedictine monastery in the state of New York. A co-founder of the inter-religious Center for Spiritual Studies, he has been active in interreligious dialogue since 1966. People all over the world have joined his network www.gratefulness.org.

Shams Anwari-Alhosseyni

Shams Anwari-Alhosseyni was born 1937 in Tehran where he passed his examination for the master diploma in calligraphy with a teaching license as the first calligrapher at the Academy of Fine Arts. In Germany, he studied medicine, oriental studies and ethnology at the University of Cologne. Until today he has been a university lecturer for Persian language, literature and calligraphy at the University of Cologne. He became a regular member of the European Academy of the Sciences and Arts. There have been numerous exhibitions of his work.